Norfolk

40 Coast & Country Walks

The author and publisher have made every effort to ensure that the information in this publication is accurate, and accept no responsibility whatsoever for any loss, injury or inconvenience experienced by any person or persons whilst using this book.

published by
pocket mountains ltd
The Old Church, Annanside,
Moffat DG10 9HB

ISBN: 978-1-907025-921

Text and photography copyright © Jo Sinclair 2022

The right of Jo Sinclair to be identified as the Author of this work has been asserted by her in accordance with the Copyright, Designs and Patents Act 1988

A catalogue record for this book is available from the British Library

Contains Ordnance Survey data © Crown copyright and database 2022 supported by out of copyright mapping 1945-1961

Printed by J Thomson Colour Printers, Glasgow

MIX
Paper | Supporting
responsible forestry
FSC® C023105

Introduction

Anyone visiting Norfolk for the first time, especially a townie or hill person, will be struck not only by the county's flatlands and big skies, but its variety too. For daytrips, weekends and holidays it's a popular destination with more to it than favourites you may already love, yet it's one of England's least populated counties. This guide explores beaches, broads, brecks, forests, fens and farmland. At times, these vast landscapes seem to belong only to the rare and spectacular wildlife as the crowds disperse. Out of season, clues and relics left by ancient settlers, monks, marsh people, weavers and merchants are sometimes the only human signs.

History

Walkers were exploring Norfolk more than 800,000 years ago. Small hollows revealed on the storm-lashed shore at Happisburgh in 2013 appeared to be human footprints. Digital analysis later proved them to be evidence of a small group of adults and children walking the mudflats of a river estuary, making them the oldest footprints outside Africa and the earliest evidence of humans in Britain. Grime's Graves in the sandy Brecks is dotted with Stone Age flint mines, regarded as the oldest industrial site in Europe. At Holme-next-the-Sea, two Bronze Age 'seahenges' were found on the beach. The Celts had a stronghold in Norfolk, with the Iceni tribe doing their utmost to fight off Roman rule. Their biggest settlement (taken over by the Romans) was at Caistor St Edmund. The Peddars Way marks the route the Romans took across the county, and examples of their forts at Warham in North Norfolk and Burgh Castle in the Broads still remain. It was the Romans who made the first attempts to drain the Fens.

In the post-Roman period, the Angles created the kingdom of East Anglia, divided regionally into South Folk and North Folk – Suffolk and Norfolk as we know them today. The Saxons and Normans left a legacy of 131 round tower churches, a Norfolk speciality – there are 659 medieval churches here. The historic hearts of King's Lynn and Norwich represent the county at its wealthiest and most populous, when trading focused on wool and weaving. In a climate that couldn't compete with the north where surging rivers helped power the Industrial Revolution, it was the Agricultural Revolution that roused Norfolk. Mined by Stone Age toolmakers for flint, Norfolk soils have supported everything from rabbit warrening in the poor Brecks to flowers, root vegetables, salad and pumpkins in the fertile Fens.

Almost 20 percent of Norfolk's modern workforce remains in the farming, food and hospitality sector. There are around 60 breweries and several vineyards. Sugar beet, malting barley, wheat, potatoes and oilseed rape proliferate, even on heavier claylands. Poultry farming has a long history here (Bernard Matthews' 'bootiful' turkey empire started with raising and processing birds inside a grand country hall). Fields of pigs rootle in the Brecks while lavender and asparagus are a speciality in loamy North Norfolk, the foodie and farmshop hotspot.

Wildlife

Norfolk offers wildlife 'spectaculars' that seem to take you back to another era, thanks to the rarity of species, as well as sheer numbers. Much of the saltmarsh, sand, shingle and heath coastline is managed as a National Nature Reserve, and the Norfolk Wildlife Trust's reserves represent the county's exciting variety of habitat and species, from reedbeds to pingo ponds.

The bulge jutting out into the North Sea is a magnet for birdwatchers. Hundreds of thousands of migratory birds make landfall here, from vast and noisy skeins of pink-footed geese arriving from Iceland and Greenland in autumn to tiny songbirds that find refuge in the dunes and pines. Wildlife thrives relatively undisturbed in the remote Broadland, Breckland heath and Fens, allowing iconic species such as the common crane to make a comeback.

Managing human and canine footfall has proved possible even at popular beaches such as Holkham, and an army of volunteers helps protect the seal colonies that are so vulnerable to disturbance. A consortium of rural estates is embracing the 'rewilding revolution', with species such as beavers reintroduced. Northern pool frogs are back in the Breckland pingo ponds, thanks to the Wildlife Trust. One of the county's original survivors is the swallowtail butterfly. In England, it is now found only in the Broads, putting this exquisite species top of the wildlife bucket list.

Walking, weather and topography

The waterbound Fens, Broads and North Sea, as well as the arid Brecks, create unpredictable weather and microclimates. Checking wind direction is a top tip for coastal walks as northeasterlies blow cold even on fine summer days. Though generally a temperate region with low rainfall, the flatlands are exposed, with nowhere to hide. 'Hill' is sometimes a misnomer referring to a sand dune or gravel hillock, but the Cromer Ridge, an ice age glacial deposit reaching 102m high, runs for 14km along the North Norfolk coast, and river valleys gently roll.

Norfolk's landscape is in flux. The Broads Authority predicts that some of Broadland will soon become saltmarsh. Receding cliffs and landslips are a feature of Norfolk's far easterly coastline (for this reason not featured in this guide), but bear in mind they tend to occur when heavy rain follows dry weather. The website tidetimes.org.uk is useful for planning walks. Keep an eye out for warnings such as car parks liable to flooding. The Royal National Lifeboat Institution warns of dangerous sandbars and fast-flowing channels, and swimmers must be wary of riptides.

It's not all perilous, of course. Walking is mostly unchallenging here on a network of almost 2000km of linear and circular routes around the county, many of them waymarked. The Norfolk coast stretches for more than 160km, most of which is accessible from the Norfolk Coast Path.

Getting around

Rumours that rural roadsigns are removed by locals is occasionally confirmed by regional newspapers. Whether it's a throwback to foiling *Dad's Army*'s enemy or a campaign against the Chelsea Tractor, who knows, but SatNav is often as baffled as you. For natural navigators, the constellations might put you back on track beneath dark skies. Two sites on the North Norfolk coast are designated Dark Sky Areas. The low population of rural Norfolk and its farmed landscape make it quite remote, but despite low traffic levels, fast cars and tractors might take you by surprise. On some quiet country roads there are signs imploring 'Slow You Down' – the local dialect, another product of a remote location, is proudly maintained. Many place names are pronounced quite unintuitively: Stewkey is Stiffkey; Potter Heigham Ham; Wymondham Wimdom; and Hunstanton Hunson.

Having no motorway helps Norfolk retain its charms, but Norwich is only 90 minutes by train from London, and King's Lynn is also on the mainline. The Bittern Line railway connects Norwich, North Norfolk and the Broads. Heritage steam railways are a way to explore the area, as well as being a nostalgic attraction. Eco coal has been trialled, but if the thought of coal-powered travel has steam coming out of your ears there's the Coasthopper bus route, Norfolk Coast Cycleway, National Cycle Network Route and long- distance walking routes.

About this guide

Throughout this book there are references to the regional long-distance paths that make Norfolk such a draw for walkers. The routes featured may only show small sections, but help to provide a perspective on how they link up across Norfolk as a whole. Times given for each walk are a rough estimate based on average walking speed of 3.5km per hour, allowing time to look at the guide and map and enjoy views and destinations.

In a county with so much water, be it seashore or watermeadow, access for walkers will always be dependent on the weather. Plan ahead, checking weather reports and external sources such as the Environment Agency and organisations' websites and social media updates. For example, Welney's fenland A1101 Wash Road is periodically cut off by floods, and high tides surge or spill onto Norfolk's Coast Path.

Areas with seasonal restrictions or dog bans are mentioned where possible and 'sensitive wildlife area' is a plea to keep dogs on a lead. Many routes cross land grazed by sheep or cattle for part of the year and walkers are advised to keep a respectful distance from cattle and calves, while always keeping any dogs on a lead.

West Norfolk is where the Brecks meet the Fens and the Wash meets the North Sea. The Fens can be an inaccessible hinterland where an infinity of drainage systems foils even intrepid explorers. Discover rights of way in this mysterious, remote world occupied only by agricultural workers and spectacular wildlife. Designated waterway routes (the Fen Rivers Way and Ouse Valley Way) lead to Denver, Downham Market and eventually the port and market town of King's Lynn.

Dress for whatever the weather might throw at you in this exposed landscape, but enjoy those big horizons. The Denver Sluice complex near Downham Market is the Spaghetti Junction of flood defences, guiding water to King's Lynn and out into the Wash. One of the richest wildlife areas in England, the Wash is a shallow, muddy estuary that attracts thousands of birds that flock and fidget in murmurations as the tides turn. Looking towards Lincolnshire between the Wash and the corner of the North Norfolk coastline is Hunstanton. This classic Victorian resort town – named Sunny Hunny, and not just because it rhymes – is the only west-facing resort on the east coast.

Old Hunstanton banded cliffs ▸

6

West Norfolk

Hilgay watermeadows

Distance 5km Time 1 hour 45
Terrain country footpaths (wet at times),
quiet lanes Map OS Explorer 228
Access buses to Hilgay from King's Lynn
and Downham Market

The friendly village of Hilgay is a
popular fishing and boating stop-off on
the River Wissey near Downham Market
and King's Lynn. This circular walk
passes fen and watermeadows 20m
below the heart of this 'island' village.
Revived by the Norfolk Wildlife Trust
and local farmers, this living landscape
is a haven linking wildlife hotspots
such as the popular Welney Wetlands
Centre 11km to the southwest. A refuge
from the bleaker expanses of the
flatlands, this leafy route is especially
enticing in summer.

From the bus stop at the East End
junction on Bridge Street, walk along East
End, keeping left where the road bends
right to Church Road. At Old Stable Yard
cottage carry straight on to join a grassy
track (Thistle Hill Road).

Hilgay and neighbouring Southery are
the only two settlements in the Norfolk
Fens recorded in the Domesday Book.
The hilly knoll of Hilgay became a Saxon
settlement, but a rich seam of
archaeology has thrown up assorted
treasures. At the start of your walk on
Thistle Hill Road, there are traces of
medieval manorial earthworks on the left.
Indicated on the OS map, this was a
moated site with earthwork enclosures
containing a series of fishponds that can
still be seen when water levels are high.

Keep going, enjoying views across the
wetlands towards the course of the River
Wissey and a long stand of poplar trees to
your left. In just under 2km, turn right at
the Norfolk County Council waymarkers

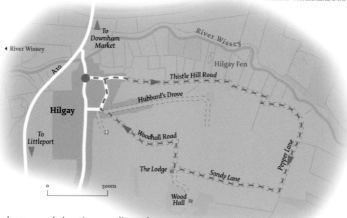

along a wooded section on a dirt track. Following the right-hand bend, Pepper Lane meets Sandy Lane, looking towards Wood Hall (just visible through the trees to your left, at which point the sandy track meets tarmac). Turn right opposite the hall entrance at The Lodge (where a public footpath can create a slight shortcut but may be overgrown).

Follow Woodhall Road to the left. This very quiet lane leads back to the village of Hilgay. You eventually reach a junction beside a pond (which is not visible in summer); carry straight on, ignoring Hubbard's Drove. Turn right on Church Road, though it's worth continuing ahead just a few paces to visit All Saint's Church. Set well back from the road up an avenue of trees, the church is associated with village inventor Captain George William Manby, who is said to have tested his revolutionary Manby Mortar nautical distress line from its tower.

Follow Church Road, keeping left beyond Green Hill to return to the start. If you want to extend your walk, Bridge Road leads downhill to a small shop and the Rose and Crown pub at Hilgay Bridge. From here, riverside footpaths take you deep into the Fens in both directions, with links to Welney Wetlands Trust and to Denver Sluice and beyond.

Welney Wetlands are well worth a visit. The visitor centre offers an immersive wildlife experience, with hides and walks, as well as indoor first-floor views over the nature reserve oasis surrounded by farmland. The Wildfowl and Wetlands Trust, along with Norfolk Wildlife Trust, protect the peatlands of the Fens for their national importance to bird conservation and climate change mitigation, wetlands being the most effective carbon sinks on the planet.

Downham Market and Denver

Distance 14km **Time** 4 hours 30
Terrain pavements, quiet lanes, country
footpaths, marshy areas; livestock
Map OS Explorer 228 **Access** Downham
is well served by trains and buses

Downham Market is a fenland town
between Ely and King's Lynn. Enjoy its
cheery clocktower, independent shops
and carrstone 'gingerbread' architecture
on your way to Denver village. Quiet
lanes, byways and marshy common pass
close to a windmill with a café and
brewery taproom. The Denver Sluice
complex is the engineering icon of the
Fens, with megalithic sluices controlling
floods and tidal surge. Get a great view
over the Ouse Washes before returning to
Downham along the river.

From Downham Station, turn left up
Railway Road. Yes, up; like most old
Fenland settlements, Downham was built
on a hill surrounded by marsh. Pass The
Green. When it's open, the Discover

Downham Heritage Centre on Priory Road
makes a good detour for market town
history dating back to Saxon times.
Otherwise continue as Railway Road
becomes Bridge Street. Little remains of
the market, but Downham exported 30
tonnes of butter per week until the 18th
century, and the horse fair was said to be
the largest in Europe.

Go up the hill to the clocktower. Turn
right along the High Street, then join
London Road. From the Royal Mail
delivery office go straight over the
roundabout, crossing to the Union
building on the opposite side and going
down Ryston End. Keep left onto Ryston
End at the end of the playing fields, then
look for a right turn next to the last house
onto Nightingale Lane. This gravel track
will take you across a bridge over the
A1122. Follow signs for Denver, going left
along Nightingale Lane, then right on
Ryston Road. At St Mary's Church, go left
onto Downham Road. Cross with care and

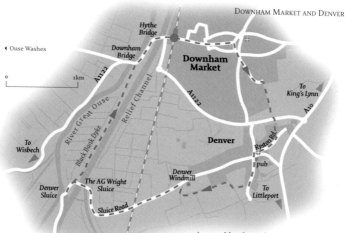

◀ Ouse Washes

Hythe Bridge

Downham Bridge

Downham Market

To King's Lynn

To Wisbech

River Great Ouse

Black Bank Dyke

Relief Channel

A1122

A1122

A10

Denver

Ryston Rd.

pub

Denver Windmill

The AG Wright Sluice

Denver Sluice

Sluice Road

To Littleport

0   1km

keep the Bell Inn on your left to go down Whin Common Road.

Where the road bends left, keep right to join a country track. At the end of the hedgerow, turn right. Go left at the next footpath junction and carry straight on to reach a green lane. You are parallel to Sluice Road, and Denver Windmill is visible through the trees as you continue to Sluice Common.

A boardwalk leads to a kissing gate. Turn right, entering a brambly common. Keep right, aiming for a red-roofed house to find the gate and exit the common. Just to the right, Denver windmill houses the Blackstone Engine Bar – the taproom of the Two Rivers Brewery, it serves award-winning beer and hosts live events. There's also a café next door.

Continuing the walk from the common gate, turn left. The lane goes over a level crossing and leads to the A G Wright Sluice. Try to get your head around the five waterways of the Denver Complex, or simply thrill at the sight of waters surging away in their race to become white horses at sea. Thirsty Cambridgeshire is desperate to hold on to more of its water, and a new Fens reservoir is on the cards.

From the A G Wright Sluice, walk through the car park and picnic area to the opposite side. Climb up the embankment for great views of Denver Sluice and the Ouse Washes rivers. Return to Downham Market either along the River Great Ouse from Denver Sluice on the Fen Rivers Way, or the Relief Channel below the A G Wright Sluice on Black Bank Dyke.

Approaching Downham you can see an enormous flour mill on the right-hand side – aim for this. Both trails lead to Bridge Road (the A1122). Turn right to join the pavement leading to Hythe Bridge and Downham.

King's Lynn

Distance 4km **Time** 1 hour 30
Terrain pavements and grass
embankment **Map** OS Explorer 236
Access King's Lynn is well served by
trains and buses. Ferry does not operate
on Sundays or bank holidays – check
other holiday times. Environment
Agency website updates River Great
Ouse flood warnings

Medieval 'Lynn' is a handsome surprise
if you know it only as a bottleneck at the
warehouses and retail parks. Leave town
via a narrow alley to catch the ferry across
the mighty Great Ouse. The west bank
gives you a fresh perspective on the
riverfront. It's an invigorating walk back
to explore architectural highlights such
as the wonderful flint chequerboard of
the town hall.

Start at Ferry Lane, a narrow alleyway off
King Street, unless arriving by car, in

which case it is best to begin this route
on the west side of the river. The ferry
service, dating back to 1285, almost ceased
in 2020 but was saved, and the crossing
remains a popular daily commuter
service. Landing at West Lynn on the
opposite bank, an information point
describes the views across to town.
Looking downriver, the modern port is in
operation. Before the 2008 recession, it
was the fastest growing port in Britain,
and it was England's most important in
the 14th century. The River Great Ouse
meets The Wash just beyond Lynn.

Walk upriver. The ferry walkway
becomes a pavement, then a grassy track
on the river embankment. Opposite a
shelter and bench you can see across to
King's Lynn Minster, which you'll pass
later. Elevated above arable fields, you're
soon looking towards the A47. Don't
worry, you won't be walking along it but

◄ Trinity Guildhall

crossing the footway of Cut Bridge. The washes to your left at the river's edge are a good place to spot wildfowl and wading birds. Beyond the roadbridge in the distance looms the Palm Paper factory.

At Cut Bridge turn left and cross the river, then turn left onto the riverbank on the Fen Rivers Way, signposted for the town centre. It generally hugs the riverside, but bear right if you need to avoid the tidal marsh at the Nar Valley Way section. Your route to the town centre is then signposted 'Waterfront, Marriott's Warehouse, South Quay'. Following the signs for South Quay, the path wiggles around Boal Quay. Keep left to cross Mill Fleet water. Take the next right onto St Margaret's Lane, then left onto St Margaret's Place, passing Hanse House. Dating back to 1475, this is the only surviving example of the medieval trading cartel known as the Hanseatic League. Turn right to arrive at the historic Saturday Market Place for King's Lynn Minster and Trinity Guildhall with its striking chequerboard flint fascia, home to Stories of Lynn, the visitor information centre. Making your way along Queen Street to the left you pass a Tudor building, Thoresby College, which originally housed the priests of the Trinity Guild.

At Clifton House Tower, two medieval merchant's houses are combined in a Tudor rebuild with an 18th-century tower. Turn left on King's Staithe Lane to rejoin the river quay and old warehouse quarter. Cross the River Purfleet and turn right to pass one of Lynn's most iconic buildings, Customs House, built in 1683.

Turn left along King Street and return to the ferry via Ferry Lane, or carry on a short way to view the Guildhall of St George. The largest surviving guildhall in England, it is said to have a continuous history of Shakespearean theatre and still operates as an arts centre today. Just beyond is the grand town square of Tuesday Market Place.

Dersingham Bog

Distance **2.5km** Time **1 hour**
Terrain **country footpaths; sensitive
wildlife area** Map **OS Explorer 250**
Access **no public transport to the start**

This fascinating stop-off on the coastal
route is a geological and wildlife gem.
Part of the royal estate, its sweeping
views of Sandringham forest, heathland
and the Wash mark the edge of what was
originally coastline. For seasonal impact,
see purple heather in high summer,
fungi in autumn and magical *Narnia*
wonderland in snowfall. Fun for children,
it has a boardwalk zigzagging into the
heart of the bog; look for the carnivorous
sundew plant.

Starting from the Scissors Car Park or
one of the forest lay-bys, enter the nature
reserve managed by Natural England.
Walk straight ahead through the woods
onto the blue waymarked trail down the
track. There's pine, oak, sycamore, sweet
chestnut and birch woodland on your left
before an area of open heath. Looking
towards the distant forest, keep to the
left-hand trail, ignoring a right turn.

You soon reach the boardwalk to the
right. This detour is a chance to scan for
species such as the fly-eating sundew. You
are looking at the largest and best
preserved example of acid valley mire in
East Anglia. The heathland on the higher
ground is also a rare survivor across East

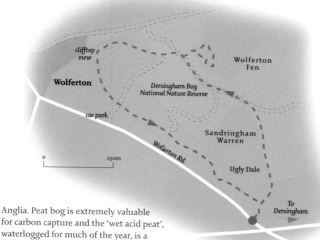

Wolferton

clifftop view

car park

Wolferton Fen

Dersingham Bog National Nature Reserve

Sandringham Warren

Ugly Dale

Wolferton Rd

To Dersingham

0   250m

Anglia. Peat bog is extremely valuable for carbon capture and the 'wet acid peat', waterlogged for much of the year, is a superb refuge for wildlife. Specialist flora in turn attracts invertebrates, and the reserve is important for heath and bog birds such as nightjar and woodcock, as well as woodland species like long-eared owls and crossbills. There's a chance of seeing the quirky territorial displays of the nightjar and woodcock on late spring evenings. The male nightjar flashes a white tail bar, churrs like a deranged machine and claps its wings loudly. The male woodcock makes circuits, croaking like a frog and finishing with a feeble whistle. Summer holidays might be a good time to try to find glow-worms, a species that can still be found here largely thanks to protection from light pollution on all sides.

From the boardwalk, turn right to rejoin the blue trail and then climb the steps on the left, signposted for Wolferton Car Park. Now join the red route to the right to take advantage of the 'clifftop' walk with views over the forest as far as the Wash. This is northwest Norfolk's greensand escarpment of the Lower Cretaceous period, called the Dersingham Formation – a geological gem that might inspire imaginings of roaming dinosaurs. It really is a unique landscape.

From the top, bear left on the sandy trail, rejoining the blue route marked 'Heathland Ramble'. Ignore the signpost to the car park on the right. Follow the path through the woods parallel to the road. Go down the steps and turn right to return to the start.

◀ Dersingham Bog boardwalk

Old Hunstanton and Holme Dunes

Distance 10.5km **Time** 2 hours 30
Terrain sandy coastal paths and quiet
lane; sensitive wildlife area
Map OS Explorer 250 **Access** buses to
Old Hunstanton from Fakenham and
King's Lynn

Unlike North Norfolk's flint and brick
cottages, Hunstanton's vernacular is
red carrstone. The Victorian and mock
Tudor holiday resort is famous for its
distinctive cliffs with contrasting bands
of red and white chalk. Beyond Old
'Hunston' the coast is a wilder place of
dunes and inaccessible creeks offering
refuge to migratory birds. Holme Dunes
on the Peddars Way is the location of
'Seahenge', one of the most significant
Bronze Age monuments ever discovered.

Start at the northeastern corner of Old
Hunstanton car park, furthest away from
town. Heading down the slope to the
beach, join The Norfolk Coast Path on the
right. Acorn waymarkers take you
between hedges, above the beach huts
and past the pines. Continue beyond the
RNLI Lifeboat Station. Following the path
at the top of the dunes, you reach and
continue beside the golf course. The path
narrows in places; you can join the higher
bank, with views over the coastal inlets.

Eventually you arrive at a solo wooden
hut near the end of the golf course.
Where the fenceline ends, turn right to
follow the Coast Path. At the junction
with the Peddars Way (which heads 74km
to Knettishall Heath in Suffolk) beside
the Norfolk Wildlife Trust information
board, turn left.

Looking out to sea beyond Gore Point,
you can glimpse Lincolnshire on the other
side of the Wash. Ignoring the next right
turn, keep to the well-defined path
curving round towards a rooftop in the
pines, the Holme Dunes Visitor Centre.

An information board marks the site

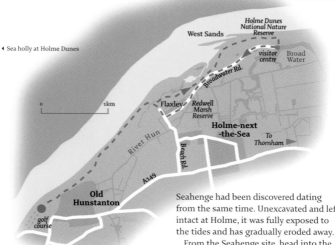

◄ Sea holly at Holme Dunes

Holme Dunes
National Nature
Reserve

West Sands

visitor
centre

Broad
Water

Broadwater Rd.

Flaxley

Redwell
Marsh
Reserve

Holme-next
-the-Sea

To
Thornham

River Hun

Beach Rd.

A149

Old
Hunstanton

golf
course

0   1km

of Seahenge. In 1998 it revealed itself as a timber circle emerging from the sand. Made from oak felled 4000 years previously, the 6.6m-diameter circle with 55 posts up to 3m high had been built on saltmarsh, protected from the sea by dunes and mudflats. Peaty soil preserved the entire structure.

Thought to have been constructed by farmers living here in wattle and daub roundhouses, it may have been ritualistic; a narrow entranceway was aligned to the rising midsummer sun. Druids and modern-day pagans were among many who protested against controversial plans to dig up and remove Seahenge. Lynn Museum now houses about half of the original timbers, with a lifesize replica of the circle on display.

In July 2014 it was revealed that a second

Seahenge had been discovered dating from the same time. Unexcavated and left intact at Holme, it was fully exposed to the tides and has gradually eroded away.

From the Seahenge site, head into the pines. Turn left for the sandy beach or right to the visitor centre with shop, café and bird hides. Return to Hunstanton from the visitor centre car park along Broadwater Road, towards a modern timber and glazed house. Konik ponies graze the marshes, which attract thousands of geese. A quiet residential road follows the course of the River Hun past Redwell Marsh Reserve, eventually meeting Beach Road. Turn right (or left if you want to visit The White Horse pub).

Passing the car park (with refreshments kiosk) and toilets, rejoin the Coast Path on the left and walk beside the golf course again. Further along, join the beach if tides allow. Before returning to the car park (at the end of the row of beach huts, this side of Old Hunstanton Lighthouse) take a look at the famous banded cliffs.

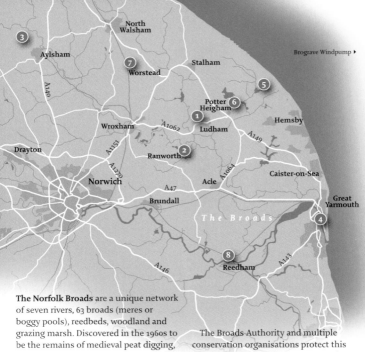

North Walsham

Aylsham

A140

Brograve Windpump ▶

Stalham

Worstead ⑦

Potter Heigham ⑥ ⑤

① A1062

Ludham

Wroxham

A1151

A1270

Drayton

Ranworth ②

Norwich

A47

Brundall

Hemsby

A149

Caister-on-Sea

Acle

A1064

The Broads

Great Yarmouth ④

Reedham ⑧

A146

A143

③

The Norfolk Broads are a unique network of seven rivers, 63 broads (meres or boggy pools), reedbeds, woodland and grazing marsh. Discovered in the 1960s to be the remains of medieval peat digging, the area has long been a boating playground. But with only 13 of the broads open to navigation year round, walkers and wildlife find they have much of it to themselves.

Few roadbridges make this a remarkably isolated place; it is said that there are people living on one side of the River Yare who have never visited the village opposite. In a landscape dotted with 74 drainage mills, walking is varied across its nature reserves, coastline, grazing marsh and inland villages.

The Broads Authority and multiple conservation organisations protect this fragile national park, home to more than 25 percent of Britain's rarest fauna and flora. The swallowtail butterfly, extinct from the rest of the UK, is perhaps its most famous wildlife icon.

Reed cutting for thatch has helped preserve the Broads as we know them; otherwise the reedbeds would have reverted to woodland. Windpumps to drain the landscape now help retain water levels, but climate change is predicted to risk inundation from the sea, creating areas of saline water and mudflats.

Norfolk Broads

Ludham and How Hill

Distance 7.5km **Time** 2 hours 30
Terrain marshy country footpaths, 200m
road section (no pavement); sensitive
wildlife area **Map** OS Explorer OL40
Access no public transport to the start

This route takes you beyond How Hill's
Environmental Study Centre and nature
trail. An unusual feature in the flat
Broads, How Hill is a knoll of glacial sand
and gravel some 15m above sea level.
More than 200 acres of reedbed and
marsh surround the grounds of a
thatched mansion and formal gardens.
Harvested annually for reed and sedge
thatching, it is home to swallowtail
butterflies, marsh harriers and bitterns.

From How Hill's public car park, cross
the lawn to find a track on the left which

is signposted for Toad Hole Cottage.
This museum, managed by The Broads
Authority, was once a marsh worker's
family home. Join the footpath to the left
along the River Ant, signposted for
Ludham. The Authority's Electric Eel boat
trips run here between April and October
(check their website for days and times).

The gravel path passes the staithe boat
moorings. Note how manicured the
neighbouring grounds are with their neat
boating lake and island of silver birches,
compared to the dense reedbeds and
marshes cut off by water. A large part of
the marsh was tamed for the formal
gardens of How Hill House but the
remainder is a Site of Special Scientific
Interest and National Nature Reserve.

Passing Turf Fen Drainage Mill on the

opposite bank you soon leave the River Ant behind, and your path becomes a grassy track following a lode. There are great views of the reedbeds and meres from the elevated causeway as you head towards Ludham. Decide now whether or not to turn left to return to the start if you need to avoid the 200m road section at Ludham village – it requires fine weather and good visibility as there's no pavement. An unmarked footpath on the left leads into the reeds and returns to the river. Otherwise, to continue, head towards the sail-less Neave's Drainage Mill in the distance, in the direction of Ludham.

You eventually reach Ludham Bridge staithe. At the road, turn left onto the pavement and follow the A1062 to Johnson Street. Beyond the houses the path peters out, but there's enough of a verge to step out of the way of traffic.

Turn left at White House Farm to follow a lane called Clint Street to Limes Farm. After passing the farmhouse on the right, go through a gate into a yard beside a barn. The track, now Blind Lane, soon bends to the right (to double back to How Hill). You're shortly looking down on the reedbeds of Buttle Marsh, a nature reserve, from the hillside. Continue on the grassy track beside farmland. Walk beyond the information board to a gate and keep straight ahead. The next gate is level with Neave's Drainage Mill and the one after this takes you into the reedbeds along a narrow peaty path. At the footpath junction, keep ahead along the waymarked trail. Arriving at a wide gate, ignore the right turn and join the main path ahead. This takes you back onto the riverside path, past the moorings and Toad Hole Cottage, to reach the start.

Turf Fen Drainage Mill

21

Ranworth Church and Broad circular

Distance 6.5km Time 2 hours 30
Terrain country footpaths, quiet lanes;
sensitive wildlife area – no dogs on
Ranworth Broad nature trail
Map OS Explorer OL40 Access no public
transport to the start

Crosscountry footpaths and quiet lanes
lead to Ranworth village and St Helen's,
the 'Cathedral of the Broads'. A fun
challenge to climb the tower rewards
with views towards Great Yarmouth. Visit
Ranworth Broad nature reserve, planning
around seasonal closures – the floating
Broads Wildlife Centre closes 31 October.

Start at the Norfolk Wildlife Trust car
park on Farm Lane, a no-through road in
Ranworth, opposite Malthouse Broad.
Turn right out of the car park to walk
along the lane past Harry Brown's
Cottage. Beyond the moorings and

grazing marsh, Dairy Farm has a thatched
barn still used for drying reed harvests.
Heading towards the trees, keep straight
on, then leave the lane to join a bridleway.

This enticing green lane with old oak,
hazels and holly trees passes open
farmland and later South Walsham Broad,
hidden behind wet woodland carr and
marshy meadows. Keep right at the bend,
now following a gravel bridleway to a
country track where South Walsham
Broad is visible.

At the lane carry straight on, ignoring
the right turn up Common Road, to pass
houses on the right, pasture on the left.
Arriving at the road, go straight on and
turn right at the next fingerpost to pass
a thatched cottage of brick and flint.
Beyond a metal gate, pass woodland and a
rough overgrown meadow marked private
land. A stile takes you into a meadow

grazed by cattle; keep to the right. At the gate by the red-roofed house climb the stile, arriving at a pond. The right of way takes you past the ancient thatched open barn, to the right of the stables. Follow the waymarker along a hedged track to Panxworth Church Road and the ruin of All Saints Tower. Turn right to return to Ranworth on a quiet road with a bit of a verge. Continue beyond the Priory Road junction and take the next right to reach St Helen's Church.

You can climb the churchtower (donation box). It's challenging but enchanting, with narrow stone steps, two ladders and a heavy trap door. The steep twisting staircase winds past flint walls, wooden beams and the church bells for views over Ranworth and Malthouse Broads, as well as Great Yarmouth in the far distance to the southeast.

Leaving the churchyard, turn right on Broad Road and pass the village hall. The entrance to Ranworth Broad nature reserve is just around the bend. The 750m of boardwalk (no dogs) through alder carr leads to open reedbeds and can be a good place to see swallowtail butterflies from late May to July. The floating Wildlife Centre, with views of Ranworth Broad, is fabulous. The only boat out here belongs to the Trust which offers boat trips. An attic in the thatched roof has a row of telescopes trained on the huge expanse of water, an excellent chance to view waterbirds such as ducks and geese, gulls and terns, and even ospreys, enormous fish-eating birds of prey. Kingfishers can be seen zooming from perch to perch around the edge.

To return to the start, follow the boardwalk out of the reserve, turning left at the road and left again. There's a boardwalk pavement on the left-hand side as you approach Malthouse Broad.

◀ Ranworth Broad Wildlife Centre

Blickling Hall Estate

Distance **7.5km** Time **2 hours 30**
Terrain **pavements and country
footpaths; livestock** Map **OS Explorer 252**
Access **no public transport to the start**

**Located between the Broads and the
North Norfolk coast, Blickling Hall has
more than 4600 acres of woodland,
parkland and farmland. Some 3km from
Aylsham on the Bure Valley Railway line,
it connects to the Weavers' Way between
Great Yarmouth and Cromer and the
Marriott's Way from Norwich to Aylsham.**

Facing the road in the main car park,
take the path left of the visitor's centre,
towards the hall. Turn right, passing the
Buckinghamshire Arms, and left along
Blickling Road, soon reaching a
photogenic view of the Jacobean mansion
framed by sculpted yew hedges. The 17th-
century moated country house was the
childhood home of Anne Boleyn. Built
on the site of a late medieval moated hall,
it is surrounded by an early 18th-century
park, elaborate gardens and a deer park.
The bequest of Blickling Hall to the
National Trust in 1940 was a pioneer of
the 'death duties dodge' that rescued
and opened up big houses and their
grounds to the public. More than 1000
country houses were demolished during
the 20th century. The National Trust Act
of 1937 and the Country Houses Scheme
enabled the first large-scale transfer of
mansion houses.

Head towards St Andrew's Church,
entering the churchyard at the corner. Exit
onto the road and cross over to join the
Weavers' Way on Silvergate Lane. Look for
the waymarker hidden in the hedge on
the right after about 400m. This takes you
into the trees, through a gate and onto

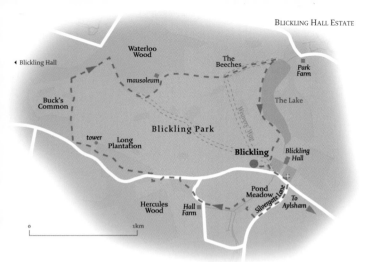

Pond Meadow with views of the hall and church. From here, aim for the small brick pumphouse. Follow the path around the sides of the wood, leading to a field-edge path going left along a hedge.

At the lane turn right, then left onto a leafy track to a cottage. The ruins just beyond were former brickworks between 1862 and the start of the Second World War. Approaching the road, take the left-hand path below. Go into the edge of Hercules Wood, then turn right to cross the road.

Joining the path beside the gateway, turn left just beyond, into Long Plantation. This passes the 18th-century tower (a National Trust holiday let). Keep to the main path. Before the road, turn right along the fenceline of Tower Park and go through the gate, aiming straight on towards the woods.

After the next gate, turn right and walk downhill beside Bunker's Hill Plantation. At the bottom turn right along the edge of the Great Wood, heading uphill with Tower Park on your right. Approximately level with the tower, turn left into the woods, following signs for the mausoleum. This 1794 pyramidal burial chamber is a little way ahead on the left. Keep to the edge of the woodland on the estate's red route. Bear right and exit the woods. Walk straight on beside open farmland with views to the Bure Valley and beyond. Keep straight ahead at the footpath junction. Aiming to join the nearest lake perimeter, turn right through a gate into the meadow to walk parallel to the water. Near the hall the path bears right, leading back to the start via a gate and the hall wall on your left. Turn left at the cottage and immediately right.

Great Yarmouth

Distance **4km** Time **2 hours**
Terrain **pavements** Map **OS Explorer OL40**
Access **Great Yarmouth is well served by
buses and trains**

Arcades, theme parks and funfairs
sprawl along Yarmouth's seafront and
are open seasonally. Hints to its heritage
as England's fifth richest town can be
seen at the River Yare's South Quay.
This walk links the two areas, passing
a Banksy mural and one of England's
most complete medieval town walls.
A smokery site, workers' cottages and
grand merchants' houses are relics of the
town's lucrative herring industry. The
fabulous pink neon Flamingoes Arcade
is surely worthy of heritage status too.

From South Beach Parade walk up
Harbord Crescent, then Barkis Road to
Admiralty Road. Banksy's artwork can be
seen above the bus stop just across

Barrack Road from the gas cylinders.
Protected by a perspex cover, it's one of 10
surviving graffiti works from the artist's
'Great British Spraycation' of 2021.

Turn right along Admiralty Road,
heading north towards St James', a
distinctive Grade II-listed church of red
brick, slate roof and cut and knapped flint.
Continuing straight on, Admiralty Road
becomes Camden Road and then
Blackfriars Road where the impressive
remains of the medieval town walls rear
up in front of you. Exploring their entire
length and archways, you'll find that the
South Tower has been renovated as a
unique holiday home. Rejoin Blackfriars
Road to visit the Time and Tide museum
near the junction of Alma Road. This fish
curing works tells the story of Yarmouth's
'silver darlings' trade, when as many as
1000 fishing boats reeled in herring hauls.
The smokery ceased production in 1988,

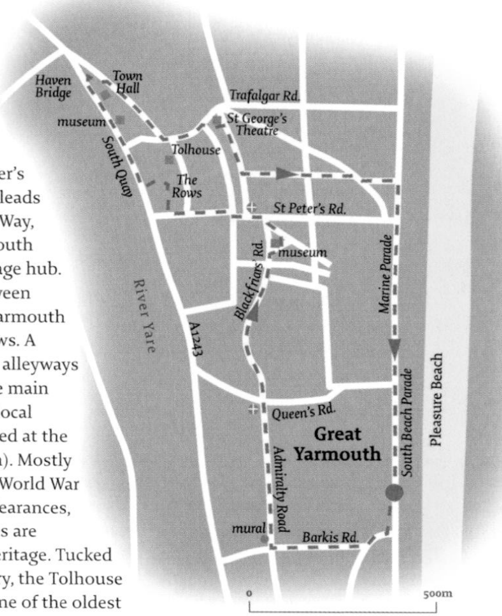

◀ Banksy mural on Barrack Road

but it is said that the aroma still lingers!

Cut through to St Peter's Road and turn left as it leads west onto Nottingham Way, towards the river and South Quay, Yarmouth's heritage hub. In the back streets between Nottingham Way and Yarmouth Way, you'll find The Rows. A network of very narrow alleyways linking the town's three main thoroughfares housed local workers (they're recreated at the Time and Tide museum). Mostly demolished by Second World War bombing or post-war clearances, two surviving properties are managed by English Heritage. Tucked behind the public library, the Tolhouse on Tolhouse Street is one of the oldest buildings in town, dating back to the mid-12th century. Originally built as a fortified merchant's house, it has been used as a prison, a town hall and a museum.

South Quay was Great Yarmouth's heart; the town was built facing the river port. On South Quay itself, the Elizabethan House museum, a National Trust property, was the home of a Tudor merchant. Keep going to the Queen Anne-style town hall. From the corner of Regent Street and Hall Plain on the east side of the hall, follow Greyfriars Way to its end where you turn left onto Yarmouth Way. Cross King Street to the baroque church-

(Map of Great Yarmouth with labels: Haven Bridge, Town Hall, museum, Trafalgar Rd., St George's Theatre, Tolhouse, The Rows, South Quay, St Peter's Rd., Blackfriars Rd., museum, Marine Parade, River Yare, A1243, Queen's Rd., Great Yarmouth, Admiralty Road, South Beach Parade, Pleasure Beach, mural, Barkis Rd. Scale: 0 — 500m)

turned-theatre of St George's. Turn right on Dene Side and left on York Road to make your way back to Marine Parade and the start. Look out for the pink neon flamingoes near The Hippodrome. Relics of Yarmouth's prosperous Georgian and Victorian resort heritage, such as the Winter Gardens, are being revived.

Beyond Yarmouth you can walk long distance on the Norfolk Coast Path, Angles Way, Wherryman's Way and Weavers' Way. Inland footpaths navigate the desolate marshes towards Norwich, and there's a Roman fort at Bergh Castle.

Horsey Mere and Beach

Distance **8km** Time **2 hours 30**
Terrain **sandy beach; sensitive wildlife
area (restrictions Nov-Jan to protect
seals); livestock; wet, muddy footpaths**
Map **OS Explorer OL40** Access **no public
transport to the start**

Starting at Horsey Windpump, this
easy-to-follow loop winds past Horsey
Mere, reedbeds and cattle pasture before
breezing along the beach at Horsey Gap.
The entire walk is a chance to see Broads
wildlife, including swallowtails, cranes
and seals. The National Trust's
windpump is worth a climb for a bird's
eye view of the waterways.

Struck by lightning in 1943, the Grade II-
listed windpump reopened in 2019,
renovated with a winding cap and turning
sails. It has superb views five-storeys up.
Before setting off, follow signs to Horsey
Mere viewpoint to see the mere from the
water's edge. If you're hoping to see
swallowtail butterflies, the wildlife garden
is a good start. They're on the wing
between late May and early July.

For the main route, join the path at
Horsey Staithe with the water on your
left. Bear right as the path leads away
from the moorings. With distant views of
the mere you're instantly immersed in
this wild place of water and open skies,
swaying reeds, woodland and pasture.

The path leads away from the mere on a
reedy path with views of fields and a tree
belt on the right. Follow Waxham Cut, the
water to your left. Look for kingfishers as
you walk towards the derelict Brograve
Drainage Mill, built in 1771, ahead. Turn
right at the mill, in the direction of the
coast and houses.

At the end, the path goes left to cross a
small footbridge over a ditch on the right.
Continue straight on towards the houses.

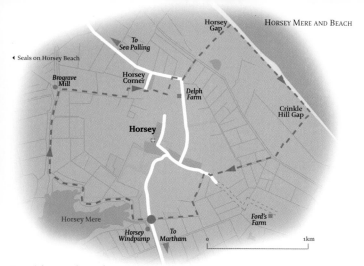

◄ Seals on Horsey Beach

*To
Sea Palling*

Horsey
Gap

*Brograve
Mill*

Horsey
Corner

*Delph
Farm*

Horsey

Crinkle
Hill Gap

Horsey Mere

*Ford's
Farm*

*Horsey
Windpump*

*To
Martham*

0   1km

Turn right onto the road at Horsey Corner and left (away from the village) to join the field edge beyond the houses. Turn left. Walking towards Palling Road, there are fields on either side of you. Turn right at the road and left onto the lane to Horsey Gap car park. Head beyond the car park to the sandy dunes and turn right.

This beach is a magnet for seal watchers, urged to keep dogs on leads and stay a good distance away. This gives the seal colony a chance to come onto the beach to rest, and to give birth. Access is restricted during the autumn-winter grey seal breeding season. Roughly half of the world's population of grey seals is found in Britain, and this is one of six locations. The smaller common or 'harbour' seal can be found among them. Despite their enormous size, (the grey 'bulls' are more than 2m long), they are all vulnerable.

A concrete walkway and tidal defence is a reminder that some of Horsey is below sea level. A tidal surge in 1938 flooded the village for four months and seawater ruined the farmland for five years. Climate change today threatens to alter the nature of the Broads if saltwater inundates freshwater broads and meres.

After 1km, you come to Crinkle Hill Gap (number 37). Climb the low barrier to join the footpath heading directly inland across the open windswept landscape of grazing marsh. Emerging at a private road, keep right towards Horsey, then go left onto a permissive path.

The path bears left before reaching a footbridge over a ditch. Cross the bridge and soon after turn right, following the ditch to Horsey Windpump. At the gate be careful of the road which is crossed to return to the start.

Potter Heigham and Hickling Broad

Distance 7km **Time** 3 hours
Terrain pavements and marshy footpaths
that flood at times; sensitive wildlife area
Map OS Explorer OL40 **Access** buses to
Potter Heigham from Gorleston-on-Sea
and Great Yarmouth

A world away from boating season
hubbub, this way to a wild expanse is
wonderful in winter. Beyond Potter
'Ham', the Weavers' Way skirts the
southeast corner of Hickling Broad.
Lose yourself to birdlife and solitude –
it's one of Norfolk's top wildlife spots,
known for winter raptors such as short-eared
owls, hen harriers and communal roosts of
marsh harriers. Heading towards
Heigham Sound, glimpses of sailing
boats come into view above the reeds.

The sign in the corner of the village hall
car park depicts a drummer boy skater
said to haunt the broads. From Potter
Heigham village hall, turn left out of the
car park onto School Road. The pavement

leads through Potter Heigham to the
quiet lane of Church Road, which takes
you to St Nicholas', one of Norfolk's 131
round tower churches. Said to be the
product of a lack of quarried stone, they
were built with rubble faced with local
flint. As well as St Nicholas' 12th-century
tower, the 15th-century brick front is
unusual. Inside there's a hammerbeam
roof, and 14th-century wall paintings.

Continue on Church Lane with the
church on your right. Join the bridleway
on the right, shortly bearing left between
hedges to head towards woodland. At the
information board, follow the path into
the woods.

After exiting the woods via a footbridge,
turn right, joining the Weavers' Way
Cromer to Great Yarmouth footpath. Your
next turning is in just over 2.5km.
Broadlands' largest expanse of inland
water, Hickling Broad, is mostly hidden by
tall reedbeds – and so are you. This screen
provides a discreet approach and you

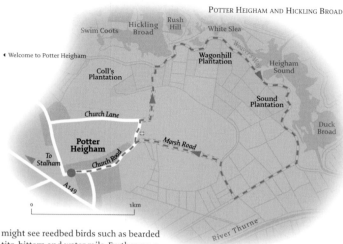

◄ Welcome to Potter Heigham

might see reedbed birds such as bearded tits, bittern and water rails. Further on, a bird hide offers a view over the water. The thatched building in the distance looking north is Whitesea Lodge, a 19th-century sporting lodge.

Owned and managed by Norfolk Wildlife Trust, Hickling Broad belongs to the wildlife, the only boat out there being the Trust's own. Seasonal wildlife tours by boat are available at the visitor centre near Hickling village. There's a tremendous sense of space here. Star species include common cranes and swallowtail butterflies. In spring there's a chorus of songbirds hidden in the reeds and leaves of the dyke, pools, meres, scrub, oak woodland and grazing marsh.

Bounce along the spongy, peaty path, avoiding the wettest areas if you can. Eventually you reach a signposted right turn. A footbridge leads to a farm track towards a small barn and distant house.

With grazing marshes to the right, look out for wildlife on the meres to the left. Extra land has been acquired here to create more reedbed, the ultimate carbon sink. Approximately in line with a derelict drainage mill, take the next right turn along the bridleway to return to Potter Heigham. Walk along a stony track with small oak trees on either side, turning left at the bottom onto Marsh Road. Continue to the end of the lane, bear left at the bend near the church and follow Church Road and School Road back to the start.

A remarkable resource that brings this landscape to life can be found online at Voices of Hickling. This oral history project by local University of the Third Age members captures living memory anecdotes of life on the Broads, from royal coot shoots to hard winters and ice skating by moonlight.

Worstead

Distance **6.5km** Time **2 hours 15**
Terrain **quiet lanes, country footpaths**
Map **OS Explorer 252 or OL40**
Access **trains on Bittern Line to Worstead from Norwich and Sheringham; the station is just over 1km from the start**

Accessible from the Bittern Railway Line, this walk follows quiet woodland lanes with parades of oak trees and old byways. The 14th-century St Mary's hints at the wealthy heritage of this fine sleepy village which grew rich from the cloth first made by Flemish weavers who settled here in the Middle Ages. Norfolk's largest village festival is held here in July.

Start at Church Plain. With your back to the church turn right and keep right, passing the White Lady pub. Head out of the village along Front Street and Sloley Road, passing Worstead Belt woodland on the left and Worstead Hall Farm and equestrian centre on the right. The quiet lane continues with woodland on both sides. Take the third turning on the left, signposted for Dilham.

A long lane of oak trees leads you along Mill Lane. Go downhill to cross the roadbridge over the river, then uphill again. Leave the road, turning left as it makes a sharp bend to the right. A hedged concrete track leads to the woods. At a private gateway turn right onto a public byway, Carman's Lane. This woodland boundary with its ditch and bank has all the hallmarks of ancient woodland and is alive with birds.

The green lane leads to a road which you continue straight over onto farmland, following the byway with a hedgeline on the right. You soon see the church and distant rooftops of Worstead village.

◀ St Mary's interior

Turn left at the next
footpath fingerpost.
The field edge path
leads to a woodland
boundary with a
lovely pond on the
left, then takes you into
a green lane. When you
reach a footpath junction
by a red-brick barn, turn
right onto a track called
Green Lane. This leads to
a high-hedged road where
you turn left. At the next
junction turn right to
return to the start.
(Alternatively, go straight
over from the barn if the
field footpath is clear.)

St Mary's, built in 1379,
was financed by the
proceeds of wool and
worsted cloth production. The
remarkable Philippa of Hainault,
Queen to Edward III, was a highly
influential political and commercial
advisor. After she advised that importing
foreign material should be banned,
Flemish weavers settled in East Anglia
and the industry boomed. Some 5km
north of Worstead, the village of Walsham
was named after the more lightweight,
summery version. The Worstead Guild of
Weavers, Spinners & Dyers is still active
here and aims to promote and share
traditional crafts.

The large church was rebuilt in the
late 14th and 15th centuries in the
perpendicular gothic style. It has a
hammerbeam roof, fan-vaulted screen
and corbels decorated with the coats
of arms of church patrons. Later additions
include a late 15th-century stepped font,
and an early 16th-century chancel screen.

The Weavers' Way long-distance
footpath is just to the north of Worstead.

Reedham

Distance 7km **Time** 2 hours 30
Terrain pavements and muddy footpaths;
sensitive wildlife area **Map** OS Explorer
OL40 **Access** trains to Reedham from
Norwich and Lowestoft; buses to
Reedham from Cantley and Acle

See the chain ferry and swing bridge in
action on this village circuit. Detour from
the river and marsh of the Wherryman's
Way to visit the church, Pettitts Animal
Adventure Park and Humpty Dumpty
Brewery. A superb hillside view from the
railway bridge looks down on Norton
Marshes where Chinese water deer graze.
Reedham has a choice of pubs, cafés and
shops. The Yare Navigation yacht Race
takes place here in September.

From Reedham Station, cross to Ferry
Road to reach the ferry in around 20
minutes. The grazing marshes are
dominated by Cantley Sugar Beet Factory.

Built in 1912, it was the first British factory
to successfully process sugar beet, one of
East Anglia's biggest crops. Plumes of
steam make it an atmospheric landmark
in winter when thousands of pink-footed
geese grazing the marshes do a fly-past.

There has been a crossing at Reedham
since the early 17th century, and the ferry
cranks into action on request. Connecting
this side of the River Yare to Lowestoft,
Beccles and Bungay, the only crossing
point between Norwich and Great
Yarmouth can slice 48km off a road trip.

Join the embankment of the
Wherryman's Way, heading back towards
Reedham, passing Wherryman's Mill (also
known as Red Mill). The River Yare is
screened by reedbeds whispering in the
breeze. Look for furtive reedbed
specialists such as Chinese water deer,
bearded tits and marsh harriers. The path
ends at a boardwalk taking you away from

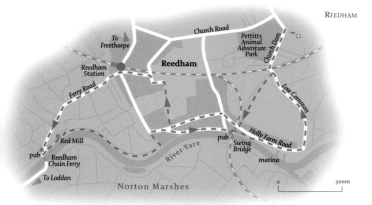

the water and into the village to the right. Continue beyond the war memorial to join Riverside with its pubs, post office and farm shop deli-café. Halls of Reedham built wherries here until the early 1900s. These sailing barges carried timber, coal, sugar beet, scrap metal, ice and tar, but only a handful survive.

Walk past The Ship pub and go under the railway bridge. Continue to the end, turning left up a lane by the last cottage. Turn right to rejoin The Wherryman's Way on Holly Farm Road (it's not a dead end, despite its appearance). Pass Reedham Marina and reedbeds (Reedham means 'homestead by the reeds'; you can still see traditional reed harvesting in action here).

Just beyond the last house on the left, turn left up Low Common. Pass the grazing marshes to reach the handsome church at the top of the hill via the railway crossing and Church Dam. In 2017 excavations at St John the Baptist proved to be the site of a Roman fort. The hill was a seaport before the land was drained.

Beyond the church, find Pettitts and the brewery shop. Ignoring the footpath signed Reedham, retrace your steps and cross the railway line. Turn right on Church Footpath above the line with views behind you to the mills and windfarms towards Great Yarmouth.

Turn right onto Holly Farm Road, with views of the swing bridge and Norton Marshes – up here you may spy shy Chinese water deer grazing on the marsh. The swing bridge carries the Norwich-Lowestoft Wherry Line across the Yare. The original 1840s' bridge allowed the passage of the tall wherries. The current swing mechanism (1903) opens around 1300 times a year.

Carry on, crossing School Hill and Middle Hill. Turn right before the war memorial onto a field-edge path (Witton Green). At the cottage, turn left and follow The Havaker parallel to the railway line, to the station. For a longer walk, the Wherryman's Way continues towards Great Yarmouth.

Nostalgia thrives in North Norfolk with its sandy beaches and harbour towns. Everyone has a favourite they'll return to forever – though 'forever' could be relatively short-term. The tidal surge of 2013 was a reminder that this coastline is fragile. Devastating the seafront, damage was compensated by a revival that hasn't robbed the area of its original charm. Availability of the perfect coffee, craft beer or sourdough hasn't seen off old-fashioned pleasures such as gilly-crabbing, candyfloss and buckets and spades. A micro-fishing industry supplies local restaurants, and seafood and samphire are sold at roadside stalls.

Vast sand and shingle beaches disperse holiday and weekend hordes. The east coast gets a battering from the elements, so this chapter includes inland walks, sheltered woodland and river valleys. Architecturally, the distinctive local vernacular is flint walls and red pantiles. North Norfolk's churches are varied and interesting, and some have the county's famous round towers.

This is one of the most important areas in England for waders, wildfowl and seals; much of the coastline is a National Nature Reserve. One of the area's most evocative experiences is the sight and sound of tens of thousands of pink-footed geese that overwinter here.

North Norfolk

Wells-next-the-Sea and Holkham Bay

Distance 10km **Time** 3 hours 15
Terrain pavements and sandy beach (hard
surface from town to Lookout café beside
the pinewoods). Check high tide times,
heed warning sirens. Sensitive wildlife
area – seasonal access restrictions to
protect wildlife; check holkham.co.uk
Map OS Explorer 251 **Access** buses to
Wells-next-the-Sea from Hunstanton,
King's Lynn and Cromer

Wells-next-the-Sea is a favourite seaside
destination, with bucket and spade
shops and busy quayside. A harbour
as far back as the 11th century, Wells
became famous for malt export in the
18th century – the story of its heritage
is told at The Maltings.

Start at the junction of Staithe Street
and the Quay (near The Maltings heritage
and information centre) in Wells. Turn left
along the Quay, following the harbour
wall to join the Norfolk Coast Path. Leave
behind the bucket and spade shops,
arcades, gilly-crabbing and the *Lifeboat
Horse* sculpture, aiming for the pavement
and causeway. Continue beside the sailing
club and saltmarsh with the water to your
right. Commercial fishing flourished here
between the 15th and 17th centuries,
bringing cod and herring from Iceland.
Modern-day businesses have bounced
back from the tidal surge of 2013 when
water levels came higher than the fatal
east coast disaster of 1953.

Keep going to reach the new lifeboat
house. Continue straight ahead onto the
sand or stay on the bank if there's an
extra-high tide. Walk along the shoreline
for firmer footing, keeping parallel with
the pinewoods towards Holkham. Bear in
mind that high tide sometimes reaches as
far as the beach huts. At low tide in high
season the beach is busy until you get

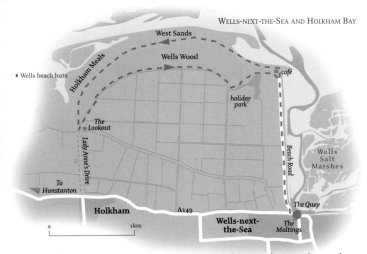

West Sands

Wells Wood

café

Holkham Meals

◄ Wells beach huts

holiday park

The Lookout

Wells Salt Marshes

Lady Anne's Drive

Beach Road

To Hunstanton

Holkham

A149

The Quay

Wells-next-the-Sea

The Maltings

0   1km

beyond the huts, opening out to the famously wide expanse of Holkham Bay. It makes a big impact, deserving of its status as one of England's top beaches.

Some 800,000 people, 500,000 cars and 300,000 dogs per year have been recorded at this National Nature Reserve. Thanks to the public heeding warnings and observing restrictions, wildlife such as rare nesting plovers and terns continue to nest behind the roped-off areas.

The pinewoods offer shelter for birds and humans from unforgiving northerly winds. Criss-crossed by public paths, they are dark overhead, soft underfoot and undulating. Planted about 200 years ago by Thomas William Coke of Holkham Hall, they're a mix of Scots, Corsican and maritime pines. The trees stabilised the dunes they were planted on, protecting the grazing marshes next door from sea and sand.

At a gap between the trees about 4.5km into the route, keep close to the pines to follow the fenceline joining a boardwalk to Lady Anne's Drive. The Lookout café, built in 2018, nestles in the landscape. To return to Wells, turn right from the café on the firm track with the woods on your left. Meander in and out of the trees and dunes, or head straight back. The path ends at a pond on the right, next to Pinewoods Holiday Park. Passing between the car park, toilets, shops and café, return to Wells on the right.

To explore further, Holkham is south of the Lookout café, beyond the end of Lady Anne's Drive. For a wonderful nature walk to Burnham, walk west from the Lookout to follow the pines (on your right), passing ponds, marshland, reedbeds and bird hides. At the end of the path, go into the woods and out the other side to pick up the Norfolk Coast Path.

Burnham Overy Staithe

Distance 10km Time 3 hours 30
Terrain country footpaths and sand;
sensitive wildlife area; car park can flood
at high tide Map OS Explorer 251
Access buses to Burnham Overy Staithe
from King's Lynn and Fakenham

The Burnhams are seven separate
parishes. Burnham Overy Staithe, a
sailing harbour with an embankment
leading to the beach and Norfolk Coast
Path, is where Horatio Nelson learned
to sail. Born nearby at Burnham Thorpe
rectory in 1758, he took command of
his first ship at the age of 20 and rose
to become Lord Admiral, despite never
overcoming his chronic seasickness.

Join the Norfolk Coast Path from East
Harbour Way in Burnham Overy Staithe.
Walk along the embankment above
Burnham Overy Creek. From this elevated
viewpoint you can see across the grazing
marshes to the pinewoods of Holkham

National Nature Reserve on the right.

At the end of the embankment (about
2km along) leave the coast path to head
left at the edge of the dunes, next to the
saltmarsh. Go into the dunes to the high
point, Gun Hill. To the right of a little
brick ruin and an old wooden moored
boat, it's well worth seeking out. 'Hill'
seems a misnomer until you climb up to
views of Scolt Head Island, the beach,
mudflats, inland villages and incoming
weather. If the weather is severe you'll
understand why rare migrant birds are
known to congregate here; the sheltered
sandy slopes interior is like the inside of
a volcano or amphitheatre. Geologists
reckon Scolt Head Island (a nature
reserve) is the best example of an
offshore barrier island in Britain. About
800 years ago it was a ridge of stones lying
in the shallow North Sea but it has been
pushed inland by north winds.

Leave Gun Hill in the direction of the

◄ Sailing boat at Burnham Overy Staithe

distant woodland, walking along the path below the dunes at the edge of the saltmarsh. You can probably make out figures walking along the embankment; head back and rejoin it in the direction of Burnham Overy Staithe. After 1km, take the left-hand path. Follow the grassy track through gateways to join the A149 ahead. Cross the road onto a stony track in the direction of Burnham Thorpe.

Soon, turn right onto the footpath, then look for a left-hand waymarker 100m along at a gap in the hedge. This takes you diagonally across the arable fields towards Burnham Overy Town, joining Gong Lane. Go downhill. The Saxon round churchtower you can see is St Margaret's at Burnham Norton, but you're heading for the church of St Clement. Turn left onto Mill Road and then right to join a green lane, or detour to visit the church on the hill, overlooking the River Burn. The church was begun in the Norman period and unusually for Norfolk it has a central tower, one of just a handful of medieval churches in the county with this layout. The original tower became unstable in the 17th century so the upper stage was removed, but it has a distinctive

bellcote and a gilded weathervane.

From the green lane you can see a windmill to the right. At a five-bar gate marked Mill House go through into the meadow above the river and marsh before exiting to Mill House. Turn right onto the road here, crossing to the footpath over a stile on the left just beyond the millpond. The hedge-side field-edge path goes up a slope to another stile. Walk in the direction of the windmill, diagonally over the field. This right of way now leads parallel to the road and takes you back to the start.

Holkham Hall

Distance **7km** Time **2 hours 30**
Terrain **pavement and country tracks
suitable for wheels, some muddy spots;
sensitive wildlife area; livestock**
Map **OS Explorer 251** Access **buses to
Holkham from King's Lynn via
Hunstanton and Fakenham via Wells**

Holkham Hall is a grand ancestral pile
sitting above marshland beside the
North Sea. The house apes the Italian
architecture that inspired a young
Thomas William Coke, the Earl of
Leicester, during a Grand Tour. He also
used the estate to promote some of the
key concepts of the Agrarian Revolution.
In Victorian times, the estate was famous
for hunting and wildfowling. Extending
to marsh, pinewoods and sandy beach,
it now incorporates England's biggest
National Nature Reserve.

From the Victoria Inn at Holkham
village, go towards the Holkham Hall
entrance. Enter the grounds at the North
Gate just beyond the almshouses. Turn
left along the path to a wrought-iron gate
into the woods. Take the second right
turn, following the green waymarkers.
The path loops round to the left, then
continues south towards more woodland,
with open farmland on the right. Watch
buzzards and red kites soaring here, the
latter sometimes gathering for communal
roosts. The network of woodland and
copses typical of the big estates was
planted to provide cover for game, as well
as supplying timber and firewood to the
hall and village. Modern Holkham aims to
be sustainable and pioneering. Seasonal
farm produce and game (this is still a
shooting estate) and venison supply the
village's Victoria Inn restaurant.

◀ Holkham Hall Deer Park

The track turns right and leads to The Great Barn. It then bears right, left and right again onto a straight avenue leading up to an enormous obelisk. This imposing, rather aggressive stone blade hints at a darker past. The Palladian-style 18th-century hall soon comes into view, master of all it surveys. Go downhill and cross a cattle grid with views of the distant coast and Coke Monument.

Walking towards the lake, have a look at the ice house on your left. Take the next right turn along the main path past the house and courtyard ticket office, gift shop and café. Large herds of fallow deer can be seen at close quarters in the deer park. Just beyond the main car parking area, turn left to return to the North Gate where you came in.

Beyond the village, Holkham Beach is part of an 18km stretch of coastline designated as National Nature Reserve. The terrestrial areas are mostly managed by Holkham Estate, while the foreshore below the high water mark is managed by government body Natural England under lease from the Crown Estate. You might be one of the 800,000 visitors per year, but you'll be amazed at the immense sense of space.

To continue your exploration of the area, you can head over to Lady Anne's Drive. For Burnham, walk west from the far end to follow the pines lining the right-hand side of the path. This passes ponds, marshland, reedbeds and bird hides. At the end of the path go into the woods and out the other side to pick up the Norfolk Coast Path. For Wells-next-the-Sea turn right from the Lookout café.

43

Blakeney Marshes and Stiffkey

Distance 4.4km Time 1 hour 30 (one way)
Terrain raised bank footpath; some wet
areas – check tides; sensitive wildlife area
Map OS Explorer 251 Access buses to
Blakeney from Cley and Cromer; option
to return by bus from Stiffkey

Quintessential North Norfolk – Blakeney
quayside has sailing boats, seal trips,
gilly-crabbing and seasonal samphire
for sale. There are independent shops
and galleries among the flint and
cobble-wall cottages. The saltmarshes
look like a watercolour in violet when
the sea lavender blooms in summer,
and the emerald samphire later turns
red. In autumn and winter, this
windswept place is alive with the
plaintive calls of wildfowl and waders.

Start where Westgate Street meets The
Quay in Blakeney. Join the Norfolk Coast
Path between the houses and saltmarsh.

Head west away from the village, beside
the sailing boats. Ignore all left turns
until Morston, with views of the wild
saltmarshes from the embankment.

Blakeney was a prosperous port in
the Middle Ages. It silted up after land
drainage and fishing access was
compromised, but the shingle, spits,
ridges, sandbars and saltmarsh created a
perfect habitat for wildlife. After the large-
scale wildfowling and the trophy hunting
of the Victorian era, the area became one
of the first places in Britain designated as
a nature reserve. The National Trust
acquired it in 1912.

To the north is Blakeney Point shingle
spit, running 6.5km between Blakeney
Harbour and Morston. It's famous for a
colony of grey and common seals (seal
trips from Morston Marsh and Stiffkey).
Numbers of around 500 increase to
5000 in the breeding season – the greys

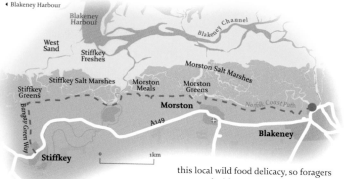

◀ Blakeney Harbour

Blakeney Harbour
Blakeney Channel
West Sand
Stiffkey Freshes
Stiffkey Salt Marshes
Morston Meals
Morston Salt Marshes
Stiffkey Greens
Morston Greens
Norfolk Coast Path
Bangay Green Way
Morston
Blakeney
A149
Stiffkey
0   1km

pup in November and December, the commons in July and August. Although it's possible to walk along Blakeney Point, the shingle is very heavy going and best left to the wildlife.

You eventually reach Morston Quay. The maze of muddy tidal creeks, managed by the National Trust, is largely inaccessible to walkers, but the oozing landscape somehow draws you in. It is mostly an avian world, supporting rare breeding waders. This group of bird species, from curlews to avocets, has a beak adapted to sifting and probing the mud for invertebrates and shellfish. Saltmarshes help control erosion, reducing the impact of the waves by as much as 95 percent. Samphire, a succulent salt-tolerant plant, covers the marsh, helping manage sea levels by anchoring silt and mud. It absorbs and stores large amounts of carbon dioxide too. It's illegal to uproot

this local wild food delicacy, so foragers go armed with scissors for a neat snip.

From Morston Quay Visitor Centre, keep left to join the Coast Path signposted for Stiffkey. Go through the coach park, keeping left of the saltmarsh, and don't cross any of the footbridges. The path splits in places, the lower path possible only at low tide. Ignore the left turn beside Stiffkey Fen. Continue to a left turn up Bangay Green Way to Stiffkey village, coming out near the church. Even the bus shelter is made of flint here. The curved red 'pantiles' so typical of local rooftops were a byproduct of the medieval wool industry when Dutch ships used them as ballast. Local pronunciation of Stiffkey as 'Stewkey' and Farrow and Ball, the heritage paint emporium, naming a paint Stiffkey Blue hints at all you need to know about North Norfolk. Stewkey Blues are the blue-toned cockles, a local catch you can buy at roadside stalls.

Retrace your steps to the start, or catch the Coasthopper bus back.

Holt Country Park and the Lowes

Distance **3.6km** Time **1 hour 15**
Terrain **country paths, some boggy areas;
sensitive wildlife area; livestock**
Map **OS Explorer 251** Access **buses from
Norwich and Fakenham stop at Charles
Road, 1.5km from the start**

Holt is a bustling little town with a
department store and food hall among
its antique, epicurean and vintage shops.
Try the Holt Owl Trail for a self-guided
tour of its Georgian architecture. Close to
Sheringham, you can travel here on the
Poppy Line railway. Holt Country Park is
a short walk away on Norwich Road. This
route circles woodland and the Lowes,
a neighbouring heathland common.

At Holt Country Park car park, face the
B1149 road entrance and turn right onto
Trafalgar Avenue, a woodland ride.
Ignoring the waymarkers, keep straight
ahead beyond the Forest School and

'amphitheatre' areas. Bear right, under an
old railway arch, and keep within sight of
the left-hand woodland perimeter. You'll
eventually see houses, near the park
boundary. Carry straight on along a gravel
footpath signposted for Hempstead. Turn
right onto Hempstead Road. Walk on the
verge for a few metres to Mackey's Hill
car park (within the country park).

From the car park keep straight ahead
past the noticeboard and map to wend
your way along a narrow trail of towering
pines and bracken. Go downhill with a
chainlink fence on the left and a stream at
the bottom. At the fork by the fence
corner, turn left up a steep slope and keep
left. Turn left on the purple waymarked
trail leading to the park perimeter. Exit
onto the heathland of Holt Lowes.

This area of heathland, bog, fen and
woodland is a 'Poor's Allotment' dating
back to the 1807 Enclosure Act. National

◄ Gorse at Holt Lowes

removal of commoners' rights was given small compensation in areas of less valuable land such as heath and fen. Locals qualifying as 'the poor' were given rights at sites such as Holt Lowes for pasture and firewood. Here, they would have collected gorse and heather. As the need for grazing and fuel declined by the end of the 19th century, the use of the Lowes became largely recreational. Rabbits, fires and military use maintained an area of open heathland and today it is grazed by horses and cattle.

Keep straight ahead through gorse and heather. Tread carefully; you may be lucky enough to see basking adders, but they're extremely shy. These rare reptiles with the distinctive diamond pattern are usually seen between March and October.

The path winds to the right. A left fork goes towards birch woodland. Although subject to change through grazing and habitat management the taller gorse forms a bit of a tunnel, taking you to an area of holly and broadleaf trees. Keep to the left to follow the path with pinewoods to your left on the outer perimeter and broadleaf trees on the inner. Stay with

the path as it winds away from the woodland on higher ground. Becoming narrow in places, it heads back towards the country park above boggy areas that are superb for dragonflies and other insects. Pass a magical mossy wet woodland as the path turns peaty. Keep left. You may hear the road as you head back to the woods, entering the country park at the pond. This beautiful glade, perfect for a picnic spot, is spectacular for its plantlife and general biodiversity.

Follow the green and red markers to return to the car park, or you can simply walk parallel to the road at the woodland perimeter (against the oncoming traffic).

Little Walsingham

Distance 4.5km **Time** 1 hour 30
Terrain pavements, surfaced paths,
country lanes **Map** OS Explorer 251
Access trains to Walsingham from
Wells-next-the-Sea on Wells &
Walsingham Light Railway; buses to
Little Walsingham from King's Lynn,
Fakenham and Hunstanton

Unless you're one of the 4000 Catholic
and Anglican pilgrims Little Walsingham
receives each year, you could feel you're
on a film set as the processions pass.
The picturesque medieval village has
a tearoom, inn and farm shop. Winter
snowdrop pilgrimages to Walsingham
Abbey grounds are popular too.

Start at Friday Market, off the High
Street. From the Black Lion pub, turn
right up Station Road. Go straight on at
the crossroads of Coker's Hill and Black
Lane. The old railway station is now
St Seraphim's Russian Orthodox Chapel
and Icon and Railway Heritage Museum.
Turn left into the coach park here to join
the old railway track signposted the
Pilgrim's Way. The Great Eastern Railway
line from East Dereham to Wells-next-the-
Sea ran here from 1857 to 1964. This
permissive path is a relaxed alternative to
the traditional Holy Mile, which has fast
traffic as well as barefoot pilgrims.

Carry straight on, ignoring a sharp left
turn. Cross the bridge above Stanton's

ALL WHO COME HERE WILL FIND HELP IN THEIR NEED

Track, a farm lane. About 10 minutes further on, at the end of the surfaced path, turn left briefly onto a concrete track to reach a crossroads. Turn right onto the lane. The Slipper Chapel ahead of you leads to the sprawling complex of the Roman Catholic National Shrine of Our Lady.

Walsingham welcomed pilgrims from 1081, but there was a hiatus after the Dissolution of the Monasteries. Incidentally, Henry VIII was the last monarch to walk the Holy Mile. Surrendered in August 1538, the Priory of Walsingham fell into ruins. The derelict 14th-century Slipper Chapel (so named because pilgrims left their shoes here to walk the last mile) was rescued at the end of the 19th century and bequeathed to a Roman Catholic order, reviving the pilgrimages once again.

For a circular walk turn right as you leave the Slipper Chapel. Follow Barsham Road, ignoring all turns until you join Fakenham Road, bearing left to return to Little Walsingham. The quiet lane follows the banks of the River Stiffkey some of the way, passing a potential picnic spot at a humpback bridge and ford. Just beyond the junction with Blind Dick's Lane, you pass a Franciscan friary on the left. Founded in 1347, it's now part of a private residence incorporated into the ruins. Keep left to return to Friday Market off the High Street where you started.

Walsingham Abbey (near the start) is the site of the original medieval shrine, the Priory of Our Lady of Walsingham. Established when the Virgin Mary appeared to the Saxon lady of the manor in a vision in 1061, Walsingham became even more important than Canterbury as a place of pilgrimage. The abbey ruins lie in 20 acres of woods, garden and parkland. The carpets of snowdrops still enjoyed here used to be harvested and sent to market by train.

◀ Little Walsingham shrine

Sheringham

Distance 8km **Time** 2 hours 30
Terrain cliffs, farmland, pavements;
livestock **Map** OS Explorer 252
Access Sheringham is well served by
buses and trains

Loved for its faded Victorian splendour,
Sheringham has charms beyond the
concrete lip running along the seafront
rebuffing the North Sea. Pebbles give
way to sandy beaches and rockpools at
low tide, and the vintage Poppy Line
links the town to Weybourne, Kelling
Heath and Holt. The National Trust's
Sheringham Park is a vast hilly park
with formal gardens, drawing the crowds
for Humphry Repton landscaping with
lavish rhododendron and azalea displays.

Start at The Esplanade in Sheringham.
Facing the seafront, turn left, ignoring the
archway, to walk west along The
Esplanade, passing the model boating
lake and concrete planters with their
cheerful bedding plants as you continue
to the RNLI Lifeboat Station. After the
Coastguard Lookout at Skelding Hill,
follow the cliffs on the Norfolk Coast
Path for just over 1.5km, passing the golf
course before a left turn takes you
across National Trust land towards
Sheringham Park. You can see a barn on
the right, and woodland beyond. This is
where steam train fans wait for the train
and wave as it goes under the bridge;
listen for the toot as it approaches. There
are views further on too as it puffs across
the landscape.

Turn right when you meet the A149
beyond the railway bridge. Cross the road
and follow the sandy track past the woods

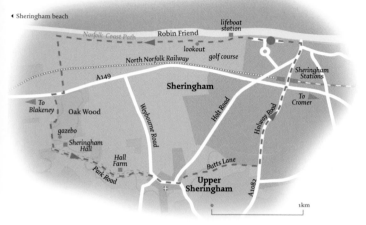

◄ Sheringham beach

lifeboat station

Norfolk Coast Path   Robin Friend

lookout

North Norfolk Railway   golf course

A149

Sheringham Stations

To Blakeney   Oak Wood

Sheringham

Holt Road

Holway Road

To Cromer

gazebo

Sheringham Hall

Weybourne Road

Hall Farm

Park Road

Butts Lane

Upper Sheringham

A1082

0   1km

towards Sheringham Park. Look out for the old pillbox on the left, built in the Second World War to ward off invasion. Around 18,000 were built around the British coastline. Sheringham made an unfortunate claim to fame in the First World War when it became the first place in Britain to be attacked by Zeppelin bombing raids in 1915, though luckily no one was killed.

Further on in the woods there are steps detouring up a slope into the treetops of Oak Wood where there's a picnic bench, as well as a wooden gazebo tower which, when open, is worth the climb for its vertiginous views over the coast. Rejoin the path to find the entrance to the park just beyond. Go through a gateway and follow the path on the left, aiming for Upper Sheringham. Sheringham Hall, a private house, is to your left; but the parkland, designed by Georgian landscape gardener Humphry Repton, is managed by the National Trust. Their visitor centre and café is at the opposite end of the park.

Go downhill and up again to follow the 'Main Drive' path out of the park over a cattle grid. Passing cottages on Park Road, continue beyond the church along The Street. Ignore Sheringham Road sweeping left and continue straight onto Cranfield Road before shortly turning left onto Butts Lane.

The footpath takes you all the way to the A1082. Turn left to walk 1km back along the pavement to Sheringham town centre where you can explore the Blue Flag beach, seafront and Sheringham Museum, with its insights into the town's fishing heritage.

Salthouse

Distance **10km** Time **4 hours**
Terrain **pavements, country footpaths,
heavy shingle; sensitive wildlife area**
Map **OS Explorer 251** Access **buses to
Salthouse from Weybourne and Wells**

**A high ridge with sea views offers a
contrast to saltmarsh and shoreline as
you loop around and above Salthouse
before a refreshing plod along heavy
shingle. The village name is derived from
the medieval salt-panning industry
which funded the improbably large
church. With a mosaic of habitats and
nature reserves, this route promises
something special all the way.**

In Salthouse, head up Purdy Street as
far as Catriona Court where a footpath
sign points left to a gap between the
magnificent flint barns. Take the narrow
path to the church on the hill. To the right
of St Nicholas', exit the driveway onto the
lane. Turn right out of the village. Just
beyond the last house, find the steps up
the bank on the left. Take a diagonal
across the field. At the top, look behind
you for views of the church, looking out
to sea. Emerge from the hedge onto
Bloomstile Lane. Turn left, following the
lane round to the top of Pinfold Hill.

This is part of the Cromer Ridge, formed
at the end of the last ice age, when the ice
sheet nudged to a halt, depositing sand
and gravel as it melted. Salthouse Heath's
mix of acid dry heath, acid grassland,
scrub and broadleaf woodland attracts
specialist biodiversity and rare species.

Walkers into archaeology might like to
detour south to Three Farthing Hill where
late Bronze Age barrows are marked on
the OS map as tumuli. There are 11
Scheduled Ancient Monuments here.

From Bloomstile Lane at the top of
Pinfold Hill, find a sign that directs you

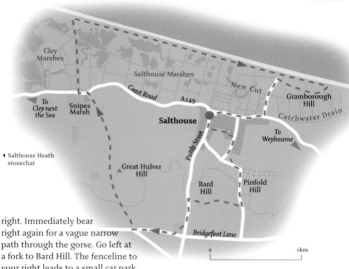

Cley
Marshes

Salthouse Marshes

Coast Road   A149   New Cut

To
Cley next
the Sea

Snipes
Marsh

Gramborough
Hill

Catchwater Drain

Salthouse

Purdy Street

To
Weybourne

◀ Salthouse Heath
stonechat

Great Hulver
Hill

Bard
Hill

Pinfold
Hill

Bridgefoot Lane

0   1km

right. Immediately bear
right again for a vague narrow
path through the gorse. Go left at
a fork to Bard Hill. The fenceline to
your right leads to a small car park.
A kissing gate on the way leads into
a paddock with grazing goats and the
ruins of a Second World War radar station.
Exit left onto the lane. Turn right at the
next footpath into the woods before
arriving at a tarmac lane where you turn
right. A footpath on the right just before
a T-junction takes you to the crest of the
hill, then back down towards the sea,
bearing left to Snipes Marsh pool (or right
for a shortcut back to Salthouse).

Turn left at the A149 and join the right-
hand footpath to the sea. This is part of
Norfolk Wildlife Trust's Cley Marshes
Nature Reserve (their excellent visitor
centre, with lookouts over the marshes,
a café, shop and events venue, is located
just before Cley village).

Turn right along the shingle, aiming for
the Second World War pillbox overlooking
a saline pool. If you've had enough, take
the footpath back to the A149 and
Salthouse village. Otherwise aim for
Gramborough Hill, worth the effort for its
slight elevation and views. Take a break
from the shingle if the tide is out by
walking on the sandy shoreline. From the
'hill' you can see the car park to the west;
reach it from the edge of the mudflats and
grassy track to Beach Road. At the end of
Beach Road turn right alongside the A149.
Narrow verges make it easy enough to
walk beside the road past some ponds to
return to the start. The church soon
comes into view and there's pavement for
the last stretch, just beyond Cross Street.

Felbrigg Hall and Sustead

Distance **8km** Time **3 hours**
Terrain **country footpaths, short section
of quiet country lane; livestock**
Map **OS Explorer 252** Access **no public
transport to the start**

This Jacobean hall between Cromer and
Holt has inviting footpaths beyond the
walled garden, dovecote and orangery.
Not far from the Norfolk Coast Path, the
Weavers' Way passes right through the
park on the final leg of its 98km trek from
Great Yarmouth to Cromer. This circular
walk passes the hall on the way down to
the lake, going through woodland and
across farmland to reach the round tower
of Sustead's medieval church.

From the National Trust car park at
Felbrigg Hall, look for the Weavers' Way
waymarkers leading to the 17th-century
hall. Going in the direction signed
'Church and Lakeside Walks' just before

the hall, head downhill. At the cattle grid
turn left. The lake comes into view and
the path leads to steps, over a footbridge
and through a gate. Keep straight, then
bear left into the trees, aiming for the lake
again via a gate and second footbridge
into wet woodland. At the end of the lake
the path goes right, into the beechwoods,
on the Weavers' Way.

Go right at the fork in the path. Head
to the road, turning right, then left a few
paces along. Join the restricted byway,
a pleasant old track edged with bracken.
Oak trees guide you along to reach a
house and pond on your left. Along the
driveway you'll see a second house and
moat. At the road turn left opposite
Brantham Cottage. Ignore the first
footpath along the narrow country lane.
Look for a second fingerpost opposite a
lane and turn left. Go diagonally across
three arable fields to Sustead church.

◄ Felbrigg Hall

The 14th-century St Peter and St Paul's was built on the site of an 11th- or 12th-century church. The round tower was built onto the west wall of the earlier building. Turn right to visit the church, then return to Felbrigg, retracing your steps through the small field behind the church. Leave the Weavers' Way, walking directly ahead across the field via a kissing gate, a bridge over a stream and a second kissing gate. Walk straight ahead on the diagonal field footpath up the hill. Turn right in the middle of the field (just before the pole where overhead cables join). When you reach the road, turn left and go uphill. At the T-junction beside the field centre in the Victorian school building, cross the road to re-enter Felbrigg Park at Gamekeeper's Cottage.

A track through the wood leads down to the lake. Pass the lake on your left, then bear right to walk uphill between two fields. Beyond the boardwalk, go through the gate on the left after the flint wall, crossing a corner of the meadow to the next gate. Aim for the church, following a diagonal path across the parkland back to the start. It's said that the church, originally in the centre of Felbrigg village, was stranded here on its own following relocation of the village due to the Plague. Another theory is that Enclosure was to blame, with parish land seized by the hall.

On the opposite side of the A148 from Felbrigg Hall there are footpaths to the coast, passing the Roman Camp and Beacon Hill, Norfolk's highest point. Its height (105m) is thanks to a glacial deposit which created a gravel ridge that stretches for 14.5km along the coastline.

Binham Priory

Distance 7km **Time 2 hours 30**
Terrain crosscountry footpaths, quiet
roads, livestock. Beware steep drops at
ruins Map OS Explorer 251 Access buses
to Binham from Wells-next-the-Sea

An imposing stone church and priory
ruins nestled within a walled meadow
are the start of this walk with hill views
across the North Norfolk countryside.
There's local real ale at the Chequers Inn
on the scenic village high street, and raw
milk on tap at the local dairy, where the
traditional milk-pail has been updated
with a self-service vending machine.

The spectacular ruin is part of a living,
breathing place; the western end of the
church survived the Dissolution of the
Monasteries. Retained for parish use it
remains so today and has been the
location of concerts, plays and Gay Pride
events. The ruins give an idea of the
original size of the wealthy Benedictine
Priory, founded in 1091.

Enter the graveyard in front of the
church. From the rear of the church, exit
to the ruins of the Chapter House where
a gate leads into a walled meadow called
The Precinct. Aim for a stile on the far
east side. Go left onto Stiffkey Road, cross
the river at Carroll's Bridge and walk up
the hill. Ignore the footpaths off to the
right; follow the road to the left and leave
it where it bends sharp right. The gravel
track to the left, Haystack Lane, takes you
over the hills with views to the south.

Keep ahead to pass a barn conversion.
Continue straight on at the stile,
following the hedge and fence. Aim for
the line of trees on your left where you

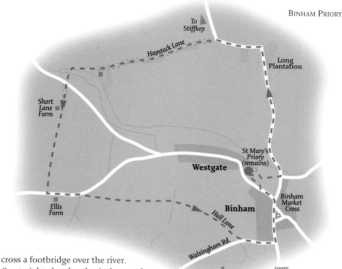

To Stiffkey

Haystack Lane

Long Plantation

Short Lane Farm

St Mary's Priory (remains)

Westgate

Binham Market Cross

Ellis Farm

Binham

Hall Lane

Walsingham Rd.

0   500m

cross a footbridge over the river.
Go straight ahead and exit the meadows
at a gateway in the hedge. Cross the lane
to continue up the hill past Short Lane
Farm. Stay on the country track until you
reach a lane. Turn left. Just past Ellis Farm
at a bend in the road and field entrance,
find the footpath to the right (the sign
might be hidden in the hedge). Cross the
field, leaving the hedge behind you.
Beyond this path, you join a green lane
heading back to Binham village. The
priory soon comes into view.

Go straight downhill, ignoring the
private left turn. You'll see the village
houses ahead. At the road, turn left on
Front Street. Just before the methodist
chapel, detour down Field Dalling Road to
The Green where you'll find the Market
Cross on your left. It's one of the best
remnants in Norfolk of a medieval

standing cross. The mortared flint rubble
base is 2m high with a shaft built from
Barnack limestone, but the stone cross
is missing, lopped off by the iconoclasts
of the 16th and 17th centuries. Market
crosses served as places for preaching,
public proclamation and penance, and
for defining rights of sanctuary. They
also marked boundaries, and sometimes
commemorated battles. An annual fair
and a weekly market was held at this
Saxon settlement from the early 12th
century, and fairs were allowed on the
green until the early 1950s.

Return to the start via Front Street,
passing the Chequers Inn. Turn left onto
Warham Road. Enter the priory meadows
via the gate in the flint wall.

Glandford

Distance 5.5km **Time** 2 hours
Terrain country footpaths; sensitive
wildlife area **Map** OS Explorer 251
Access no public transport to the start

From a cluster of rural businesses, join
the Bayfield Bird Walk. This off-road
route devised by the Birdscapes Gallery
offers rolling countryside in the Glaven
Valley, taking you through woodland and
handsome estate parkland, along the
River Glaven to the Shell Museum. The
varied habitats appeal to a variety of bird
species enjoying shelter and food
provided by woodland, farmland and
water. Ask at Birdscapes or Cley Spy for
their leaflet describing birdlife you might
find along the way.

From Cley Spy, follow the track west,
between the fields and up towards
the woods. At the start of
the track there's a clue
that the estate was
commandeered for

Second World War activities, when
Bayfield was used as a base for the Home
Guard. Several concrete Blacker Bombard
or 'Spigot Mortar' anti-tank weapon and
machine gun mountings survive.

At the top of the hill, turn left before
the cattle grid. Go up a track with pines on
a hill to the right. The woodland edge
track soon opens out to a stretch of open
farmland with views from the highest
point. To the north is Wiveton Down, part
of the glacial ridge above the coast. The
path goes into the trees of Summer
House Hill Plantation, then follows the
woodland edge, bearing left (to the west
is Langham churchtower) and left again,
downhill. Eventually you meet a lane.
Turn left for about 30 paces, then cross
to follow the footpath sign on the right.

Walk up a slope past veteran oaks.
The path opens out onto a wide
track as you head downhill.
Follow the edge of Hull
Wood. Ignoring paths

Glandford

Oulton Hill

museum

Cley Spy

River Glaven

Summer House Hill

Summer House Hill Plantation

Ladies' Hill

To Langham

B1156

Banham's Hill

Bayfield Hall

To Sharrington

Hull Wood

0   1km

to the left marked private, bear left until you meet the Blakeney Road. Cross straight over. The path to the left takes you parallel to the road, with views of the hall and lake to your right. Exit the parkland at a kissing gate in the far corner near the road. Join the path in the woods, turning right to the head of the lake via a footbridge over the River Glaven. At the estate road turn right to find the wildflower garden centre on the left. There's also a café in a timber-built Second World War billet hut.

Now turn left into the car park under the trees. Go through a kissing gate into a field with glimpses of the River Glaven; follow its course across the pasture towards the churchtower. Join the riverside in the field corner; you can see houses ahead. Exit the field on a narrow path above the river. Turn left, taking you to the footbridge over the millpond, a tranquil spot. Carry on to St Martin's Church. The Dutch gabled building in the grounds is the Shell Museum, which is open from Easter to October. This cabinet of curiosities is Norfolk's oldest purpose-built museum and has the finest seashell collection in England, alongside miscellaneous delights, from birds' eggs to random objects to archaeological finds.

The church was in ruins by the year 1730. Sir Alfred Jodrell inherited Bayfield Hall at the end of the 19th century and rebuilt it in memory of his mother. The interior's woodwork includes the end of a pew carved with a copy of Landseer's painting of a dog mourning at his master's coffin. The stained glass is by Kempe and Bryans, the best known stained-glass studios in the 19th and early 20th centuries. In the clocktower a carillon of 12 bells plays hymns every three hours between 6am and 9pm. A different tune is played each day and church services carry on regardless. Continue to the road and cross over to the shops where you began.

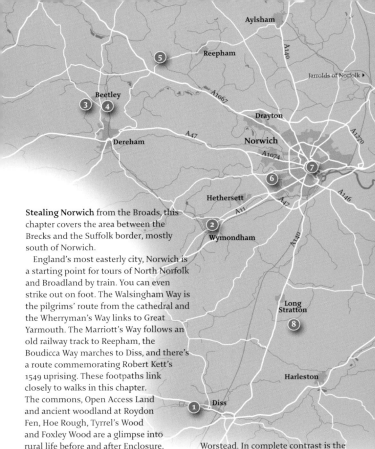

Stealing Norwich from the Broads, this chapter covers the area between the Brecks and the Suffolk border, mostly south of Norwich.

England's most easterly city, Norwich is a starting point for tours of North Norfolk and Broadland by train. You can even strike out on foot. The Walsingham Way is the pilgrims' route from the cathedral and the Wherryman's Way links to Great Yarmouth. The Marriott's Way follows an old railway track to Reepham, the Boudicca Way marches to Diss, and there's a route commemorating Robert Kett's 1549 uprising. These footpaths link closely to walks in this chapter. The commons, Open Access Land and ancient woodland at Roydon Fen, Hoe Rough, Tyrrel's Wood and Foxley Wood are a glimpse into rural life before and after Enclosure.

Norwich, which was the largest walled city in Europe by the 15th century, was the heart of Norfolk's medieval wealth and culture, but wool heritage can be seen even in small country villages such as

Worstead. In complete contrast is the University of East Anglia's forward-thinking Modernist campus and the Sainsbury Centre, where the arts, from ancient to contemporary, help put Norwich on the cultural map.

Mid and South Norfolk

Roydon Fen

Distance **2km** Time **1 hour**
Terrain **wetland, exposed tree roots;
sensitive wildlife area – dogs on leads**
Map **OS Explorer 230** Access **buses and
trains to Diss, 1.5km from the start**

On the Angles Way in the Waveney
Valley, Roydon Fen is well connected in
both directions. It's on the Norfolk-
Suffolk border, handy for Bressingham
Steam Museum and Gardens and
Banham Zoo. An enticing boardwalk
leads through woods to reedbed
clearings with views of wildlife such as
warblers and dragonflies. This
waterlogged and isolated spot has a
sense of profound calm and wildness
despite being close to town.

Step into the woods and onto the
boardwalk from the Suffolk Wildlife Trust
car park at Roydon Fen. This is alder carr,

wet woodland on peat. You soon reach an
open area of reedbed. Now managed by
the Wildlife Trust, this commonland
harks back to a threadbare subsistence.
Signs of human activity, such as flint
tools found here, date back 10,000 years.

Look out for wildlife such as summer
dragonflies, reed warblers and cuckoos.
In the woods again, the first right gives
you a look at another reedbed area.
Retrace your steps to the main route. The
distinctive winding path eventually leads
to drier woodland that could be good for a
picnic or for sitting quietly to spot birds
such as tits, finches and woodpeckers.

At the Angles Way signpost, continue to
the right. Exit the reserve to the left
through a kissing gate. Passing a house
on the bank above you, turn right onto
Roydon Cul De Sac to return to the start.
The row of cottages, aspirational in

‹ Common frog at Roydon Fen

today's property market, was once described by the writer Roger Deakin as 'East Anglia's skid row' with its 'squatters' cottages, thrown up overnight on common land'. Deakin lived not far away at Mellis Common, and the Waveney Valley's commons, river and fens are referenced in his books, which include *Notes From Walnut Tree Farm* and *Waterlog*.

West of Roydon Fen, the Angles Way joins the fascinating Commons Walk, continuing the theme of commons heritage in this corner of East Anglia. Wortham Ling, just south of Bressingham Steam, is an expanse of dry heathland

contrasting with waterlogged Roydon. The 150km Angles Way from Great Yarmouth is one of the best waterside walks in Britain. Linking the Broads to the Brecks, it follows the Waveney Valley, finishing at Thetford.

Diss is Norfolk's most southerly town. Built on a hill above a six-acre spring-fed mere, it's a member of the Slow Town movement. Originating from Italy's Cittaslow way of life, 'slow food' and local character is celebrated and quality of life encouraged – though possibly a hard ask in one of the most intensively farmed areas of the country.

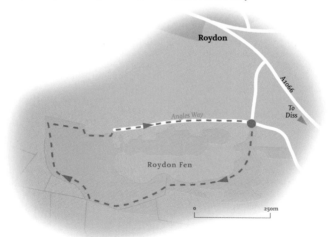

Wymondham

Distance 5km **Time** 1 hour 45
Terrain pavements and narrow riverside
footpath; ha-ha in abbey grounds with
steep drop **Map** OS Explorer 237
Access Wymondham is well served by
buses and trains

**Dominated by the abbey, this market
town 19km south of Norwich has a
mainline train station, as well as being
on the Mid-Norfolk heritage line to
Dereham. The octagonal timber-framed
market cross on stilts points the way to
the seasonal Heritage Museum, telling
Wymondham's story of Saxon riverside
settlement, medieval wealth, civic
rebellion and prison reform.**

From the information centre at the
Friday Market Place, walk along Market
Street with Queen Street to your left, then
turn left down Damgate Street. Turn right

at the bridge past a riverside residential
area. The footpath through Becketswell
Park has views of the abbey on the right.
Founded in 1107 on the site of previous
Saxon occupation, it became one of East
Anglia's most important religious houses.
A dispute between parishioners and
Benedictine monks over rights of use
lasted for centuries, but it has served as
the parish church since 1539.

Exit the park (formerly a timber stack
for one of the town's biggest employers,
the Briton Brush Company). Cross
Becketswell Road, named after Beckets
Well, a spring that attracted medieval
pilgrims. Join the River Tiffey footpath.
Narrow and overgrown in summer, it's
fairly well-trodden, with boardwalks in
the muddiest parts. Kingfishers and water
voles thrive here. You'll eventually cross
the Mid-Norfolk Railway line, then the

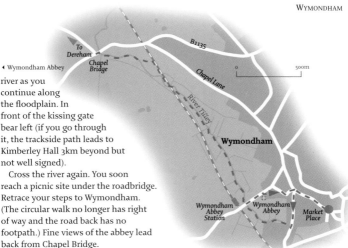

river as you continue along the floodplain. In front of the kissing gate bear left (if you go through it, the trackside path leads to Kimberley Hall 3km beyond but not well signed).

Cross the river again. You soon reach a picnic site under the roadbridge. Retrace your steps to Wymondham. (The circular walk no longer has right of way and the road back has no footpath.) Fine views of the abbey lead back from Chapel Bridge.

Turn left up Becketswell Road to enter the abbey grounds. Inside there are 200 human-sized angels in the intricate 15th-century roof timbers. There's an ornate Georgian Chippendale-style organ case, and a gilded Gothic altar screen was added in 1919 as a First World War memorial. Exit onto Church Street, passing the Green Dragon at the top. This late 15th-century building is the oldest tavern in town and a survivor of a disastrous town fire in 1615.

Like many East Anglian towns Wymondham was a wool town – 600 handlooms were recorded in 1836. A wood-turning industry also operated, and brush making thrived as late as the 1980s. But there was civic unrest in this prosperous place. In 1549 Robert Kett, a wealthy yeoman farmer, led a rebellion of peasants and small farmers in protest against the enclosure of commonland that profited from sheep farming for the weaving trade. They seized Norwich for six weeks until overpowered by 10,000 troops. Robert and his brother William were hanged (William from Wymondham Abbey's west tower). Kett's Oak, fenced behind wrought iron on the road to Hethersett, commemorates the rallying point for his march to Norwich. Local place names and community buildings honour Kett's attempt to protect rural livelihoods.

Another attempt at social justice was more successful after prison reformer John Howard declared Bridewell prison in Wymondham to be one of the vilest prisons in the country. He influenced its rebuild in 1785 and it now houses the Heritage Museum.

65

Gressenhall

Distance 7km **Time** 2 hours 30
Terrain crosscountry paths, quiet lanes
(no pavements), village streets
Map OS Explorer 238 **Access** buses to
Litcham Road, Gressenhall from
Dereham and Fakenham

Part of the Nar Valley Way, linking
Mid Norfolk to King's Lynn in the west,
this walk follows ancient byways across
farmland and through rural villages.
It's close to the seasonal Gressenhall
Workhouse Museum on the Nar Valley
Way which also links to the Wensum Way.

With your back to Gressenhall Post
Office cross to Bittering Street. Continue
along this quiet village road to the
crossroads. Turn left onto Longham Lane,
then right onto the Nar Valley Way after
100m. This leafy track has an ancient
atmosphere, with its mix of holly, hazel
and bracken. Some byways like this are all

that survive of ancient woodland, with
old oaks along the hedgelines and
bluebells that pop up annually, like a
historical flashback.

Pass a pond before reaching open
farmland. The pond might have been a
watering hole for livestock driven along
here; the next hedged section of wider
track looks like a drove road. The open
farmland is typical of Mid Norfolk,
producing sugar beet for East Anglia's
sugar factories, barley for breweries and
wheat for bread and biscuits.

From the pond, the hedged track leads
to Stoney Lane. Turn right and go
straight over the next road to soon pass
Vale Farm. Turn left at the crossroads
onto Church Lane, with its high narrow
hedges. Cross the B1146 Fakenham Road
to Field Lane. You'll eventually see the
churchtower of St Mary Magdalene.
At the end of Field Lane turn right onto

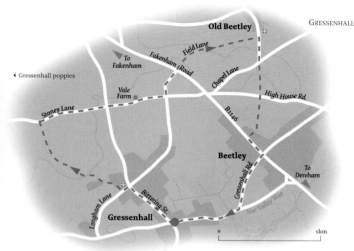

Old Beetley

Field Lane

Fakenham Road

To Fakenham

Chapel Lane

High House Rd

Vale Farm

Stoney Lane

B1146

Beetley

To Dereham

Gressenhall Rd

Nar Valley Way

Longham Lane

Bittering St

Gressenhall

‹ Gressenhall poppies

0   1km

Church Road. Keep straight on, crossing Chapel Lane at the traffic island and then High House Road before picking up the footpath signposted between the fields. Walk towards the trees and houses. Go into the woods, keeping slightly right to exit beside the school playing fields. Turn left onto Fakenham Road, crossing to join the pavement opposite before going right onto Gressenhall Road. Turn right at the next junction, following Litcham Road back to the start.

The trail marked The Workhouse and Nar Valley Way refers to Gressenhall Farm and Workhouse Museum of Norfolk Life nearby. A kinder and more welcoming place now, this forbidding building interprets the brutal reality of rural working life in the past. The 'House of Industry', opened in 1777, now houses a seasonal museum exploring the lives of former inhabitants and local farming life.

There are temporary exhibitions and permanent displays, as well as 50 acres of grounds and a working farm. Rare breeds such as the Suffolk Punch and British White cattle are a symbol of a lost way of life, where mechanisation replaced working horses and more productive farm animals were bred to supply food on an industrial scale. The Suffolk Punch, a heavy horse breed, still ploughs the workhouse land today.

From the workhouse you can also pick up the 19km Wensum Way, much of it alongside or close to the river that gives the trail its name. The Wensum Way links the Nar Valley Way at Gressenhall with the Marriott's Way at Lenwade.

Two of Norfolk's 150 lost villages can be found in the area, one at Little Bittering just northwest of your route, and remains can be seen at Godwick near Tittleshall on the way to Fakenham.

Beetley and Hoe Rough

Distance 3km **Time** 1 hour
Terrain wetland and woodland country
paths, livestock; sensitive wildlife area
Map OS Explorer 238 **Access** no public
transport to the start

In the village of Beetley, Hoe Common
and the Norfolk Wildlife Trust's Hoe
Rough reserve make an interesting
meander through a variety of landscapes.
The watermeadows, contrasting with
woodland and a small patch of heath, are
fascinating for their wildlife, but they
also offer a sense of human history.
Insights into lives on village estates,
farms and commons is told in the
exhibitions and objects displayed at the
seasonal Gressenhall Farm and
Workhouse Museum nearby.

From the small Norfolk Wildlife Trust
car park next to the roadbridge in Beetley
village, go through the kissing gate into
Hoe Rough. Keep left to follow the

Whitewater river. Narrow 'trods' wind
around this patch of grassland seasonally
grazed by cattle. Springs and variations in
the acidity and dampness of underlying
soils have created ideal conditions for rare
grassland plants, including five species of
orchids: early marsh, common spotted,
Southern marsh, green-winged and
twayblade. If you've never seen wild
orchids before, visit in May to June to find
these exquisite flowers in all shades of
purple and pink, white and green.

Valued for being one of the finest
remnants of wet unimproved grassland in
Norfolk, new land was acquired in 2020
with the hope of linking the two sides of
the river by a footbridge, as well as
doubling land held by the Norfolk
Wildlife Trust for wildlife and recreation.

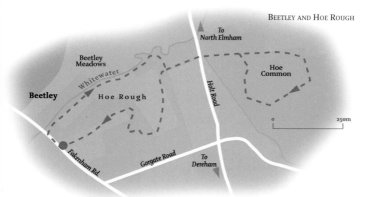

Beetley Meadows on the opposite bank has several picnic benches at a delightful bend in the beautiful Whitewater river. This tributary of the River Wensum that flows to Norwich is known for its classic chalk stream fauna such as mayflies, brown trout, white-clawed crayfish, otters and water voles.

Modern-day nature reserve management aims to increase and enhance valuable habitats by focusing on how to link them up. The Wildlife Trust has an ongoing project in Mid Norfolk to restore river corridors, and this is a perfect example, creating ecological links between isolated nature reserves through working with neighbouring landowners and increasing the size of existing reserves when opportunities arise.

A contrasting landscape can be found beyond the northeast corner of Hoe Rough. From the river and fenceline a gateway leaves the wetlands. A small strip of woodland leads to Holt Road. Cross straight over into the woods and follow the track around the perimeter of the heathland. Hoe Common is a little blast from the past. This small area of Open Access Land was allocated to the villagers as part of the Enclosure Act in 1811. Its typical heathland features such as gorse and heather would have been used for fuel, animal fodder and bedding. Heathland species such as adders can be found, as well as butterflies that visit the heather flowers. The woods are great for fungi forays, and between here and Hoe Rough the local birdlife has plenty of choice for food and shelter.

Keep to the perimeter of Hoe Common, passing close to private properties to loop back to the track in the woods. Return to Hoe Rough via the track you came in on. From the gate into Hoe Rough keep left, taking you through the wet meadows and a small area of woodland before arriving at the car park at the start.

Across the road from the car park, Mill Lane has signposts pointing you in the direction of the Wensum Way, linking to the Nar Valley Way, if you wish to extend your route.

Foxley Wood

Distance 3.5km **Time** 1 hour 30
Terrain gravel paths, country footpaths;
sensitive wildlife area – no dogs
Map OS Explorer 238 **Access** no public
transport to the start

**This secluded wood is worth seeking out
as Norfolk's largest example of ancient
woodland. It's a favourite for a
springtime bluebell pilgrimage (from
mid April to early May) and other
seasonal wonders.**

Start at car park 1, off Themelthorpe
Road, on the west side of Foxley Wood.
The wood is 25km northwest of Norwich
and 7km west of the handsome market
town of Reepham, famous for its three
churches. It's also about 1.5km west of the
long-distance Marriott's Way between
Norwich and Aylsham.

From car park 1, walk into the woods,
arriving at an information board in front
of you. Turn left, setting off along the
gravel path waymarked green. Keep to the
trail – it's all too easy to get lost, even
though it's not a huge area. The tracks
look almost identical and the trees are
dense, with tangled undergrowth. It's a
good opportunity to try experimenting
with some basic natural navigation skills.
Orient yourself according to which way
the sun is shining or the wind blowing.
Note clues such as areas of shade or
varying temperature and moisture. For
example, frost on one side of a molehill
suggests that the cold side faces north,
while open flower petals on one side of
the track indicate you're facing south if
those on the opposite side are closed.

Turn left again and walk as far as you
can to the end where the path goes right.
Turn right again and go into the middle of
the woods via a narrow path and gate to
see 'Wood Glade'. Retrace your steps to

◀ Foxley Wood bluebells

rejoin the path you were on before and turn right to continue. Keep straight on. Turn right before going right onto the broad main ride, a working area with piles of timber. The wider areas offer a good chance to see woodland wildlife out in the open, such as sparrowhawks, buzzards and jays. Other birds to look out for are nuthatches, treecreepers and woodpeckers searching the tree trunks and branches, and songbirds such as warblers and thrushes among the leaves. The wood's mixture of broadleaf trees, pines, hazel coppices and flora and fauna are typical of woodland worked for centuries to provide timber, fuel, charcoal and fencing.

Spring flowers that flourish here are primroses, wood anemone, early purple orchid, bluebells, herb-paris, lily of the valley, dog's mercury, water avens and butterfly orchid. A profusion of meadowsweet and fleabane billows along the edge of the rides later in the year. The flora attracts a good range of insects, including rare butterflies such as the silver-washed fritillary, white admiral and purple hairstreak.

Turn right at the next junction, following the clockwise markers. Before the end of the track, look for the exit trail on the left, then join the gravel track to the right to return to the start.

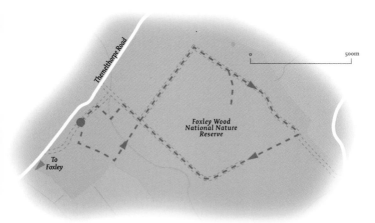

Sainsbury Centre and UEA Broad

Distance 3km **Time** 1 hour
Terrain muddy riverside paths
Map OS Explorer 237 **Access** buses to the
Sainsbury Centre from Norwich

In the grounds of the University of East
Anglia, the Sainsbury Centre is a major
contemporary gallery and art and
anthropology museum. Housed in Sir
Norman Foster's mid-1970s 'hangar', it's
surrounded by the Brutalist architecture
of Sir Denys Lasdun's student campus.
The grounds extend to 350 acres, with a
woodland, river and lakeside wildlife
trail, as well as a sculpture trail.

Sculpture trail maps and parking permits
are available at the Sainsbury Centre
(closed Mondays). From the Henry Moore
sculpture opposite the Sainsbury Centre
car park, turn left. Going down the slope
towards Anthony Caro's *Goodwood Steps*
sculpture, note Lasdun's glazed ziggurat
housing blocks inspired by ancient

Mesopotamia's terraced compounds.
Follow the curve of the Sainsbury Centre
basement windows to the right.

Head for the rear end of the Sainsbury
Centre past the red Vladimir Tatlin helter
skelter-style tower. Tatlin was one of the
most important figures in the Soviet
avant-garde art movement of the 1920s.

Hop into the woods beside the bronze
human-bunny *Rabbit Bodhisattva of Mercy*
by Leiko Ikemura. Multiple paths criss-
cross the woods. Follow a steep path
downhill to find an information board
and Yare Valley waymarkers. Alternatively,
a woodland track between the bronze
Head by John Davies and Norfolk
Road/Chancellors Drive leads to a
signposted wildlife trail for 'Earlham
Park'. Head southwest to pick up the Yare
Valley Walk downriver, signposted Eaton.

Among the 5793 different species of
plant and animal recorded within the
grounds is the elusive otter. The areas of

◄ *Rabbit Bodhisattva of Mercy*

meadow, woodland and marsh on the edge of Norfolk's Broadland district were once quite impassable. UEA Broad was dug out for gravel and sand extraction in the construction of the university.

Partly screened as you walk along the riverbank, there are playing fields across the river to your right. You emerge at a junction at UEA Broad. Turn right, passing a bridge which mimics the Mathematical Bridge at Queen's College, Cambridge, as you walk with the lake on your left and the river on your right. Approximately halfway along its south side, look across the lake to spot one of Anthony Gormley's rooftop figures. About as far along on the riverbank side is Laurence Edward's *Man of Stones*, a prehistoric-

looking bronze figure laden with flints found on site. Follow the lake perimeter all the way back to the start, finding more sculptures along the route.

The Sainsbury Centre could enthrall you all day (and has a café and shop). Robert and Lisa Sainsbury donated their art collection to the university in 1973, continuing to add to it thereafter. Spanning 5000 years of culture, the collection features European modern masters, such as Henry Moore, Francis Bacon, Albert Giacometti and Pablo Picasso. Art from Oceania, Africa, the Americas and Asia, as well as the ancient cultures of Egypt, Greece and Rome, represent a fascinating timeline of culture and art.

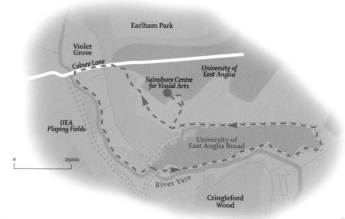

Earlham Park

Violet Grove

Colney Lane

University of East Anglia

Sainsbury Centre for Visual Arts

UEA Playing Fields

University of East Anglia Broad

0   250m

River Yare

Cringleford Wood

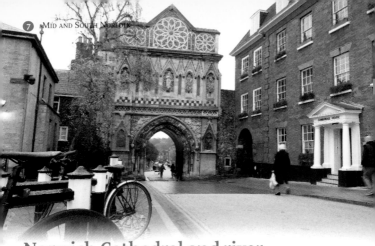

Norwich Cathedral and river

Distance 2.5km **Time** 1 hour
Terrain city streets (some cobbles)
Map OS Explorer 237 or city map from
information point at The Forum
Access Norwich is well served by buses
and trains

**This short heritage walk to the river and
cobbled streets of Elm Hill and Tombland
starts at Norwich Cathedral. Built by the
Normans, it has a 96m spire, home to
nesting peregrine falcons. Passing the
city's oldest trading post to arrive at The
Lanes, explore the newest independent
shops cheek by jowl with traditional
businesses such as Jarrold, the
department store founded in 1770.**

Starting with the cathedral lawn to your
left, walk down The Close (an area of 44
acres and 80 listed buildings). Pass the
Chapter Office and playing fields. Norwich

Cathedral is the largest building in
East Anglia and dates back to 1096, but
in fact there are two cathedrals. On the
city centre's western edge, the Roman
Catholic cathedral by Gilbert Scott is a
fine example of Victorian Gothic. The city
emerged from a Saxon settlement called
'Norvic'. Developed after the Norman
invasion of 1066, it became one of the
biggest walled cities in Britain.

Approaching the river you'll see a
medieval stone building with a wide
archway. Pull's Ferry was a crossing point
for the River Wensum, and a slipway and
watergate joined what was once a canal
linking to the cathedral site to supply
French limestone for its construction.

Walking with the river to your right, you
soon reach Bishop's Bridge. Built of stone
in 1340, it's one of the oldest bridges in
England still in use. Beyond the Red Lion

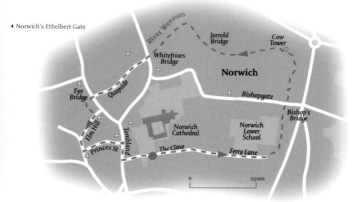

◄ Norwich's Ethelbert Gate

pub, the Cow Tower at St James' Meadow was attached to a Benedictine monastery as a tolbooth, then converted to military use as a defence tower.

After Jarrold Bridge, St James' Mill looms behind a bank of weeping willow trees. The River Wensum supplied the dominant textiles industry. Weaving, knitting and dyeing peaked in the 1720s, with 12,000 looms and around 70,000 workers. St James', built in 1839, was a textiles mill until 1901 when it became a chocolate factory. Norwich was also known for shoemaking, brewing and printing. Jarrold established a printing business here in the 19th century. Jarrold's working printing museum relocated to Blickling Hall in 2021. Colman's Mustard, located south of the city centre, produced its last batch of bright yellow pots in 2019.

Whitefriars Bridge, rebuilt in 1925, is the site of St Martin's Bridge dating back to 1106 but rebuilt several times. In 1549 it was destroyed in an attempt to prevent Robert Kett's rebellion against the enclosure of commonland. From Whitefriars drop down to Quayside to return to the city centre past a row of colourful houses. This is the oldest part of Norwich and the site of the first river crossing. Boats sailing between here and the North Sea loaded and unloaded cargoes of wool (the main export) and imports from China, America and the West Indies, as well as coal from England and fish from the coast.

Cross the road at Fye Bridge to the Ribs of Beef pub. A passageway behind the pub wends round to cut through to the cobbles of Elm Hill. Turn right, then left onto Princes Street. Keep going to Tombland. In its medieval prime Norwich was England's second largest city, and Tombland was its heart. Turn right, then left down through the ornate Ethelbert Gate to the start.

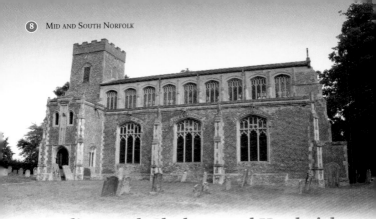

Tyrrel's Wood, Shelton and Hardwick

Distance **9km** Time **3 hours 15**
Terrain **narrow lanes – stay visible!**
Country footpaths, livestock; sensitive
wildlife area Maps **OS Explorer 237 & 230**
Access **no public transport to the start**

Surrounded by intensive agriculture,
pockets of ancient woodland like Tyrrel's
Wood stoke the imagination. Running
through it, the Boudicca Way between
Diss and Norwich is roughly parallel to
the old Roman 'Pye' Road, now the A140,
and celebrates the Iceni warrior queen's
march against the Romans.

From the car park on Wood Lane enter
the woods. Spot the Boudicca Way
markers and aim for the northside, left-
hand perimeter of the wood. Boardwalks
and stepping stones improvised from logs
guide you through the muddiest areas.
Exit the woods along a narrow brambly
hedgerow path beside farmland. This
becomes an oak tree green lane. Turn

right at Parker's Lane and right again, past
Wood Green South farm on a grassy track.
Pass the back of some houses and a row
of cottages on Wood Green common. Turn
left to keep to the Boudicca Way past a
farmhouse with red-brick barns. Follow
the edge of the common past a thatched
cottage, turning right at the next
waymarker and passing a small fishing
pond. This might originally have been a
farm pond, used for watering animals and
cleaning carts and ploughs. Nationally
rare, they are better preserved in Norfolk.

Turn right just before Mayfield Farm.
Cross an arable field, aiming for the trees
and hedge ahead before turning left at the
gap to follow the hedge to the lane. Cross
straight over. The oaks here are a typical
feature of Norfolk's narrow rural lanes.

Take either path at the fork on the
meadow. One edges around the farmland,
another is a green lane. Both emerge at a
grassy track between arable fields. Aiming

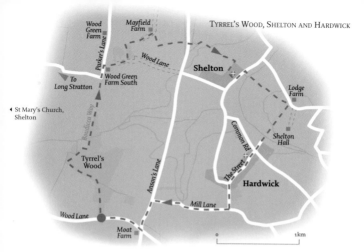

Wood
Green
Farm

Mayfield
Farm

Wood Lane

Shelton

Parker's Lane

Wood Green
Farm South

To
Long Stratton

Boudicca Way

St Mary's Church,
Shelton

Lodge
Farm

Common Rd

Shelton
Hall

Tyrrel's
Wood

Anson's Lane

The Street

Hardwick

Mill Lane

Wood Lane

Moat
Farm

0   1km

for Shelton Church, look for a bridge across the ditch towards the end, leading to the back of the Old Rectory and church.

St Mary's is an architectural treasure. In contrast to the familiar flint vernacular, most of this church has a Tudor design of red brick with stone dressings, embellished with a diaper pattern of darker bricks. It's a superb example of the Perpendicular style in a rural location. Rebuilt by Sir John Shelton of Shelton Hall, the 14th-century tower and the west window of the south aisle are all that remain of the original church.

Sir John Shelton was connected to the court of Henry VIII as he was married to Anne Boleyn's aunt. Legend has it that when Anne Boleyn was executed, her young daughter Elizabeth was hidden in this churchtower to avoid her arrest by court conspirators. Remaining under the care of Lady Shelton and her husband

she grew up to be Queen Elizabeth I.

Exit the churchyard, joining the lane to the left. Opposite the old school climb a stile into a pasture. Cross the footbridge and walk straight on towards the trees. Go through these to a stile. Keep ahead, then aim for the right-hand corner of the field (ignoring the stile crossing into woodland on the left). Head straight on from the gap in the hedge across two fields. Exit the arable field over a footbridge into a green lane. From the tarmac lane, cross Common Road to The Street. St Margaret's Church, said to be Saxon in origin, lost its tower to a storm in 1770.

The Street leads you through Hardwick village before you go left onto Mill Road. The narrow country lanes here are quiet but fast, with farm machinery also on the move. Turn right at the T-junction for Mill Lane, left on Anson's Lane and finally right to return to the start on Wood Lane.

Flat horizons with belts of twisted Scots pine, pock-marked Neolithic flint mines and pingo ponds are all part of Breckland's unique landscape. Covering 1000 sq km of forest, heathland and farmland across South Norfolk and North Suffolk, the 'Brecks' offer remote walks, fascinating history and rare wildlife.

Lucrative medieval rabbit warrens later gave way to forest when this arid landscape was planted up after the First World War to create Thetford Forest, the largest lowland pine forest in Britain. Unfertile sandy, flinty soil also succeeded to vast military airbases, but conservation projects help protect the Brecks as one of Britain's most biodiverse areas. Some 28 percent of the UK's rarest organisms can be found here. Many, like the stone curlew, thrive behind military razor-wire and free-range pig fields, others are protected at nature reserves such as East Wretham Common.

With its 400 pingo ponds, a geological ice age phenomenon, Thompson Common nature reserve at Stow Bedon has an almost primeval atmosphere, while the Roman Peddars Way, priory and castle ruins at Thetford and Castle Acre and medieval wall paintings at North Pickenham are all clues to Breckland's more anthropocentric and populous past.

Breckland

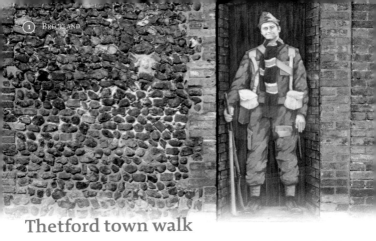

Thetford town walk

Distance 4km **Time** 1 hour 30
Terrain pavements **Map** OS Explorer 229
Access Thetford is well served by trains
and buses

**Thetford has a surprisingly rich heritage.
Founded as an Iron Age fort, it was
variously an Iceni stronghold, the
ancient capital of East Anglia and one of
the largest priories. The statue of warrior
queen Boudicca may drive her chariot in
London, but Thetford has a bronze
Captain Mainwaring from *Dad's Army*.**

From Thetford Station, turn left down
Station Road towards the town centre.
Turn right onto Miller's Lane and left onto
St Nicholas Street. Cross to Water Lane
towards Thetford Priory. Head into town
from Water Lane to Minstergate via the
underpass. (Minstergate is home to the
Charles Burrrell Museum,
commemorating Thetford's history for
traction engine manufacturing.) Turn

right onto Bridge Street. At the bridge,
drop down to the riverside footpath
where fans with selfie sticks keep the
Captain Mainwaring statue company.
Follow the riverbank to the footbridge,
crossing right to Butten Island and
the Maharajah Duleep Singh statue.
Inheriting the title Maharajah of the Sikh
Empire at the age of 5 but deposed by the
East India Company, Singh was exiled to
Britain. In 1863 he bought the 17,000 acre
Elveden Estate near Thetford with British
government funds.

Exit the island to the right and cross
a footbridge. Turn left, signposted
Nuns' Bridges, and follow Spring Walk
downstream. This area was the site of the
1819 spring house and pump room (a relic
of Thetford's spa town heyday 1818-1838),
a paper and pulp mill and a coffee mill.
Reaching Nuns' Bridges Road you're on
the Icknield Way, one of the oldest routes
in the country.

◀ Dad's Army mural, Thetford

Nuns' Bridges is also the location of Thetford's Iron Age origins. It is one of the most ancient settlements in Norfolk and claims the warrior Queen Boudicca as one of its own, being an important base for the Iceni tribe. It became the Saxon capital of East Anglia, and as the sixth largest settlement in the country at the time of the Domesday Book it was an ecclesiastical centre with its own cathedral.

(You could extend your walk from here on the scenic route to Nunnery Lakes and the British Trust for Ornithology's nature reserve, in the direction of Barnham: about 1.5km each way.)

To return to town follow Nuns' Bridge Road with the war memorial on your left. Cross the river. Turn right at Ford Street and keep going until you see a footpath next to the Castle Lane sign on the left, leading up to the Norman castle mound. The largest earthwork of its kind in East Anglia is second only to Silbury Hill in Wiltshire in size. Iron Age defence ramparts built by the Iceni tribe succeeded to a Norman motte and bailey castle built after the Norman conquest. It's worth the steep climb for distant views of the surrounding Thetford Forest.

Head into town to the left, along Rampart Way and then Guildhall Street. The Dad's Army Museum is signposted at Cage Lane. At Market Place bear left and then right to join King Street, where you'll find the Leaping Hare visitor information centre. Further on, a gilt statue honours Thomas Paine. Born in Thetford in 1737, he lived in America, becoming a radical thinker and controversial writer, the author of the *Rights of Man*. His work was hugely influential in both the American and French Revolutions.

Turn right on Whitehart Street, past the timber-framed Ancient House Museum. Continue to the top of the street to return to the railway station, crossing London Road to Station Road.

Thetford to Brandon

Distance 15km Time **5 hours (one way)**
Terrain **pavements and country footpaths**
Map **OS Explorer 229** Access **trains to
Thetford from Cambridge, Ely and
Norwich; return by train from Brandon**

**Follow the beautiful River Little Ouse to
Brandon and catch the train back. The
trail through Thetford Forest leads to the
lovely St Helen's picnic spot and the
Forestry Commission base at Santon
Downham. There are great opportunities
for birdwatching and wild swimming on
the way to the Suffolk town of Brandon,
once the 'flintknapping capital'.**

From Thetford Station, turn left down
Station Road towards the town centre.
Turn right onto Miller's Lane and left onto
St Nicholas Street. Cross to Water Lane
towards Thetford Priory. Follow the river
downstream with the priory on your
right. Go under the red-railed bridge past
a housing estate on the route marked

'River and Forest Walk'. Continue under
the A11 bypass, passing a fishing lake and
keeping to the narrow riverbank path.
Leave the riverside just beyond Abbey
Heath weir to follow the sandy path up
into the forest. Keep left to stay
approximately parallel to the river,
ignoring the forestry path to the right.

You'll eventually see the chimney of the
biomass power station. Just beyond the
building, look for the railway bridge to the
right. Follow the route signed 'Two Mile
Bottom', ignoring the way to Brandon
across the river. Go under the railway,
turning sharp left on a narrow sandy path.
Parallel to the rails you join a wider flinty
forest track. Beyond the archaeological
site of St Helen's Church and holy well
with open views to the left, continue
downhill. Turn left, under another railway
bridge. Directly after tiny All Saints
Church, take a sharp left on a narrow track
into the trees to St Helen's picnic site.

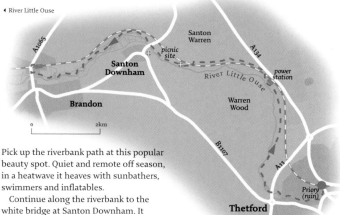

◄ River Little Ouse

Pick up the riverbank path at this popular beauty spot. Quiet and remote off season, in a heatwave it heaves with sunbathers, swimmers and inflatables.

Continue along the riverbank to the white bridge at Santon Downham. It featured in Brit sitcom *Dad's Army*, and fans like to pose here for photos. Cross to the steps down to the riverbank path towards Brandon, or stop off at the Forestry Commission car park toilets (turn left, go round the corner and bear right beyond the cottages).

When Thetford Forest was planted after the First World War, Santon Downham became a tree nursery, trialled to replenish Britain's depleted timber stocks. Hardwoods such as beech, chestnut, lime and oak among the plantation pines attract rare bird species, such as firecrests, crossbills and hawfinch.

On the Norfolk-Suffolk border, the village is famous for weather extremes. In 1668 a legendary sandstorm buried the village and blocked the river. Despite the Scots pines planted as windbreaks across the farmland, the Brecks are still liable to the occasional Brecks 'blow'.

Grime's Graves Neolithic flint mines are just north of Santon and were mined for centuries, with Brandon the centre of the gunflint industry, supplying ammunition during the Napoleonic Wars; the flint was used to spark gunpowder.

From Santon, as the river becomes deeper, look out for otters. In recent years some unusually 'confiding' ones became a tourist attraction in Thetford town centre. The poplar trees along here fall like ninepins in high winds, blocking path and river, but walkers find their way round. Approaching the road at Brandon, the path meets a residential area. At the road, turn right for the railway station.

Alternatively, a circular route back to Thetford can be found from Gashouse Drove behind Aldi, off Brandon High Street in the town centre.

83

East Wretham Heath

Distance **3km** Time **1 hour**
Terrain **country footpaths, livestock; sensitive wildlife area**
Map **OS Explorer 229** Access **buses from Watton and Thetford (request stop)**

You can join this nature reserve from the Peddars Way and Hereward Way, and it's close to the Great Eastern Pingo Trail. A precious example of classic Breckland landscape, its fascinating vanishing pools are unique to the area. Between 1942 and 1970 the nature reserve was requisitioned for military training and part of East Wretham airfield; nature has mostly recolonised the concrete runways. Check Norfolk Wildlife Trust for updates such as trail closures.

From the Norfolk Wildlife Trust car park at East Wretham Heath, go straight ahead in a westerly direction towards the trees and pass through the gate into the woods. A bird hide on the left overlooks Langmere. This pool was formed at the end of the last ice age. Its water levels depend not on rainfall, but on underground water table fluctuations affecting the depth by several metres a year. Levels rise slowly in late winter and spring as the porous chalk bedrock and sands fill with water. This slow process creates the highest water levels in early summer. Once a watering hole for sheep being driven crosscountry along Harling Drove, an ancient trackway linking the Fens with the Brecks, it's an important resource for wildlife in this arid region. Watch

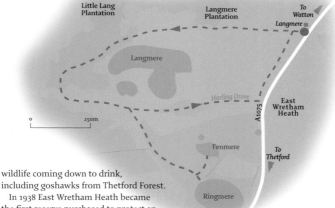

Little Lang
Plantation

Langmere
Plantation

To
Watton

Langmere

Langmere

Harling Drove

East
Wretham
Heath

A1075

0   250m

Fenmere

To
Thetford

Ringmere

wildlife coming down to drink, including goshawks from Thetford Forest.

In 1938 East Wretham Heath became the first reserve purchased to protect an area of Breckland. Commercial conifer plantations established in the 1930s devastated much of the very special Brecks ecology that had been largely untouched since Neolithic and Bronze Age wildwood clearance. 'Breckland' comes from the word 'Breck', describing exhausted land, farmed, then reverting back to heathland. East Wretham Heath is managed by Norfolk Wildlife Trust, the oldest of the UK's 46 Wildlife Trusts. As well as turf kept closely cropped by rabbits and livestock, the reserve has a mosaic of habitats supporting a range of species, such as adders in thicker cover, breeding birds like redstarts in the woods and woodlarks in the open heath, and dragonflies on the meres.

Exit Langmere hide to the left. The bracken-edged path winds through birch and pines. The beautiful twisted Scot's pines are a contrast to the plantation rows you'll see further on, and are said to have been planted at the time of the Battle of Waterloo. Follow the waymarker to the kissing gate and turn left onto a sandy track (the old Harling Drove Road). A little way along, detour through a gate on the right to visit Ringmere and Fenmere, passing oak trees to visit a Breckland meadow and a viewing point over Ringmere, another 'vanishing' pond. Retrace your steps to the main loop.

Continue on the sandy track with Langmere on your left. You can see the A1075 road ahead of you. For walks beyond the reserve, the Peddars Way between Holme-next-the-Sea and Knettishall Heath passes nearby – you can pick it up from the lay-by opposite here. To return to the start, turn left just before the road. Go through the gate and walk roughly parallel to the road.

Stow Bedon and the Pingo Trail

Distance 9km **Time** 3 hours
Terrain country footpaths and lanes, wet
areas, livestock; sensitive wildlife area –
dogs on leads at Thompson Common
nature reserve **Map** OS Explorer 229
Access no public transport to the start

Ponds, now a rarity in the British
countryside, are more common in
Norfolk than any other English county,
not least because of a geological
phenomenon known as pingo ponds.
Some 400 have been uncovered around
Thompson Common near Stow Bedon.
Enchanting and peaceful, this woodland
route and mosaic of habitats would be
great in a heatwave, for autumn colour
and fungi, or for winter wildfowl.
Summer offers a chance to spot a
multitude of dragonflies and damselflies.

Start at the Norfolk Wildlife Trust car
park off the A1075. To get there, pull into
the lay-by near Wayside Farm shop and
enter the old railway sidings driveway,
turning left immediately into the car park
at the reserve entrance. Head south from
the car park on the old railway line,
passing a cottage. Some of the smaller
pingos are visible as you walk along the
straight woodside track. From the Inuit
word for 'little hill', pingo ponds are a very
rare relic of the last ice age, formed when
subsurface ice pushed soil up into
mounds, collapsing as the glaciers
retreated and permafrost melted.

Leave the Pingo Trail as you approach
some houses, turning right onto Heath
Road. Pass Heath Cottage and keep
straight ahead through the forest. Ignore
the next forestry track to the right and,
where the track bends to the left,
continue straight ahead on a narrow
forest path leading to Watering Farm.

Beyond the farm, at the bend in the
road, turn right past a fenced-off military
firing range. This is the Peddars Way,

◀ Thompson Common pingo pond

becoming sandy as you pass gorse and bracken heathland. Beyond this is Thompson Water, a fishing lake excavated in 1854.

Take the next right to rejoin the Pingo Trail before bearing left, following the path into the woods through a kissing gate. This area of birch and holly woodland with bracken and swampy pingos is magical. A hide on the right looking over Thompson Water is a peaceful spot for viewing wildfowl and waterbirds. An iconic summer species you might see here is the hobby, a small migratory falcon. Watch out for its swift-shaped silhouette as the bird hunts dragonflies over the water.

Leaving Thompson Water behind, look for a Pingo Trail waymarker on the right to wind through the woods. All sorts of tree species – holly, hazel, oak, alder, willow and beech – create a delicious mulchy aroma in the peaty wet habitat. The reserve is host once more to the northern pool frog which became extinct here 20 years ago. One thousand of the frogs, England's rarest amphibian, have been successfully reintroduced here over a six-year period.

The path bears right, then left with the fenceline on the right, stream on the left. Cross a footbridge over the stream and bear right after a kissing gate onto an open common. The path is well-trodden enough. If unclear keep the line of oaks to your left as you cross the middle of this peaty, tussocky, scrubby area kept trim by longhorn cattle. Exit at the gate and head along a track (fenceline on your right). Continue straight on along a track with oaks on both sides. At Springfield Cottage on Butter's Hall Lane, keep straight ahead. Before you reach the junction of Church Road and Stow Bedon Road, look for a right turn from the lay-by. This leads into the nature reserve. Turn right immediately. A path winds through, picking a way between water, marsh, furze and scrub. Exit from the northeast corner via a gate and woodland path to return to the start.

North Pickenham and St Mary's

Distance 5.5km **Time** 2 hours
Terrain country footpaths, quiet lanes
and pavements, water meadows;
livestock **Map** OS Explorer 236
Access buses to North Pickenham from
Swaffham, Ashill and Necton

Not far from the market town of
Swaffham on the through-route to the
coast, this walk visits the site of a lost
village and a special church. The ruin of
St Mary's revealed its secrets in 1996
when restoration workers discovered a
series of 11th-century wall paintings.
The earliest known in Europe, they're
of international importance. With far-
reaching views from the hill, you join
the Roman Peddars Way as you descend
to watermeadows on your return to
North Pickenham.

From Pickenham Hub, the community
centre, walk into the village along South
Pickenham Road. Turn right at The Street.
Information at the village sign tells you
this was a Saxon settlement. Continue to
Houghton Lane and turn right to head
out of the village. Cross the river, passing
paddocks, houses and pig fields as the
village street becomes a narrow lane.
Turn right at the junction, onto Browns
Lane, but in under 300m leave it for a
holloway on the left, taking you uphill.
The lovely flinty track with oak trees all
the way leads to a small plateau at the top
of the hill. This is Houghton Common,
site of a medieval village, though there's
no trace of it now.

Turn right onto a footpath between
hedges. This leads to a tiny isolated
church. St Mary's belonged to the lost

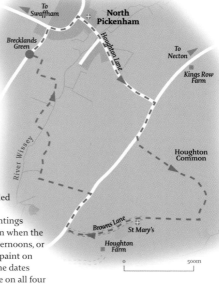

◀ St Mary's, North Pickenham

village of Houghton-on-the-Hill, located to the north of the church and west of Houghton Common. St Mary's was a long-lost ruin until a Women's Institute ramble unearthed 'signs of satanic use' there, leading to a campaign to clean it up. A churchwarden declared that Satanists were 'defiling a consecrated church' and called in the local Territorial Army unit to keep the 'devil worshippers' away. The campaign to save it from ruin led to restoration work and the discovery of medieval wall paintings in the 1990s. You can view them when the church is open on weekend afternoons, or by request. In the six layers of paint on the interior, the original scheme dates from around 1090 and is visible on all four nave walls. A second decorative layer dates from the 15th century. A third fragment shows post-Reformation text.

From the church, walk downhill past a pond. You can soon see North Pickenham and its churchtower in the distance. Where the track reaches a lane, turn right and, in just under 300m, look for a gap in the hedge on the left. Join the Peddars Way straight ahead, walking towards the distant wind turbines. This Roman road route runs for 74km between Knettishall in Suffolk and Holme-next-the-Sea.

The path bears right to cross the watermeadows that border the River Wissey as you head back towards North Pickenham. A left turn takes you through a kissing gate into the meadows and across a footbridge. The footpath follows the edge of the meadows round to the right. Exit the meadows in the far corner and keep straight on towards the village and the church. The path then bears left along a hedge (towards the wind turbines) and round to the Hub at Brecklands Green.

Castle Acre

Distance 2.5km **Time** 1 hour
Terrain country footpaths, can get
overgrown or flooded, pavement,
narrow lane **Map** OS Explorer 236
Access infrequent buses to Castle Acre
from King's Lynn and Swaffham

**Heritage and ancient ruins aren't always
catnip for kids, but these castle ruins are
fun for a run and scramble around the
mown paths, banks and bridges (beware
of heights). This short, pretty loop
leading to the priory and village is a
family-friendly walk with the banks of
the River Nar, a gin-clear chalk stream,
tempting for picnics and paddling.**

Start at the English Heritage castle car
park at the top of Pye's Lane. Castle Acre
village is a rare example of a surviving
Norman settlement complete with castle,
village, parish church and priory. The
castle, founded soon after the Battle of
Hastings, was built on the site of a late
Saxon hall. You can still drive through the
Bailey Gate (you'll walk through it later on
the walk). It's one of two stone
gatehouses added to the massive
earthwork defences in about 1200.

Stay within the grounds to follow the
Nar Valley Way downhill, with the castle
to your right. Follow the footpath behind
a hedge at the bottom to emerge onto
Cuckstool Lane. Turn left onto Bailey
Street and right at the junction onto Blind
Lane to enter the meadow immediately
opposite. Follow the path through the

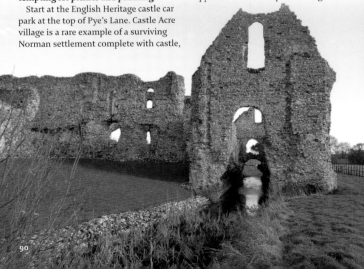

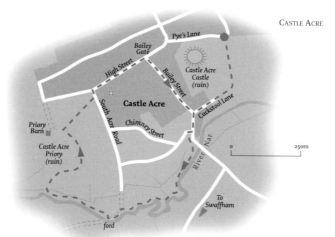

meadow along the River Nar, a perfect example of a spring-fed chalk stream. Threatened by biodiversity loss and abstraction for domestic supply, chalk streams are at risk of being lost but this one can be seen in full-flow with emerald water crowfoot, mayflies and brown trout. Kingfishers zip along the water, a quick flash of electric blue.

When you reach a kissing gate and footbridge, turn left onto the bottom of South Acre Road. This narrow lane leads to a ford and footbridge – turn right without crossing. Follow the river to the left as far as the left-hand corner of the priory meadow, then head up to the priory, following the metal railings.

The crumbling ruins represent one of the largest and best preserved monastic sites in England. It was home to the first Cluniac order of monks arriving from the reformed Benedictine order at Cluny in France. For almost 450 years it was a refuge for pilgrims and a stop-off for royalty, clergy and nobility.

Detour to St James' Church on your right or take a closer look at the priory and English Heritage visitor centre via the priory gatehouse. The large parish church is worth a look for its 15th-century pulpit and painted panels from a medieval screen incorporated into stalls in the chancel.

To return to the start head towards the High Street past Stocks Green. Walk through the Bailey Gate and down Bailey Street to rejoin the path to the castle on Cuckstool Lane.

For hiking beyond the castle you can join the ancient Roman route the Peddars Way. This national trail, 74km long, heads north from here to Holme-next-the-Sea, or south to Knettishall Heath. The Nar Valley Way, also waymarked from the castle, is 53km long and goes between King's Lynn in West Norfolk and Gressenhall in the south.

◀ Castle Acre Priory moat

Oxborough village

Distance 5km **Time** 1 hour 30
Terrain country footpaths, village streets,
quiet lanes (no pavements); sensitive
wildlife area **Map** OS Explorer 236
Access no public transport to the start

Deep within the Brecks hinterland are
two unexpectedly lush landscapes. The
National Trust's ostentatious Oxburgh
Hall, and the romantic Gooderstone
Water Gardens lure visitors off the beaten
track with their fanciful landscaping at
odds with remote country roads, flat
arable fields and weatherbeaten
windbreaker pines. This route near the
two attractions takes you along farmland
byways and quiet lanes.

Oxburgh Hall has all the enchantment
of a fairytale. The turrets are home to
purring doves and chippy jackdaws. The

walled garden, with fruit tree espaliers,
box hedges and parterres, as well as the
superb mirrored moat full of striped
perch, bring to mind *Sleeping Beauty* or
Beauty and the Beast. Owned by the
Bedingfield family, this magical place
survived periods of political peril and
brutal unrest; the Bedingfields were loyal
Catholics and served in the Royalist army.

If starting at Oxburgh Hall, turn left out
of the car park, then right, along the lane
past St John the Evangelist Church and
The Bedingfield Arms pub. Go straight
ahead to the phonebox on The Green –
there's a house opposite with a Royal Mail
postbox on its wall. Enter Church Farm
Lane here and look for the footpath sign
hidden on the right beside the hedge.
Turn right. At the stile, join the footpath
on the left by the field edge. Ignoring the

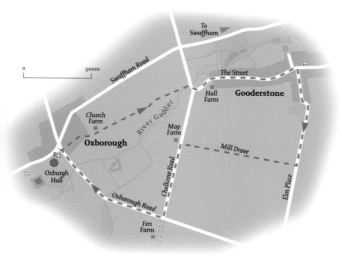

0   500m

To
Swaffham

Swaffham Road

The Street

Hall
Farm

Gooderstone

Church
Farm

River Gadder

May
Farm

Chalkrow Road

Mill Drove

Oxborough

Elm Place

Oxburgh
Hall

Oxborough Road

Fen
Farm

fishing lakes entrance, follow the hedgeline. Another stile and entrance leads across a meadow straight ahead towards trees. Follow the footpath towards the trees on the far side of the meadow, keeping left of the waterworks to reach the road. Turn right onto Gooderstone Road and cross the river.

Follow the road and pavement on into Gooderstone village, passing Gooderstone Water Gardens at The Street. Turn right onto Elm Place (just before St George's Church and The Swan pub) to walk out of the village.

In summer, birdwatchers keep their eyes peeled for the stone curlew, known to nest in the surrounding arable fields. Also called the wailing heath chicken or thick-knee, this scarce nocturnal ground-nesting bird with long yellow legs, knobbly knees and enormous yellow staring eyes is uncannily tricky to spot.

About 500m after the bend in the road beyond the houses, turn right onto Mill Drove bridleway. Follow the track to the end, then turn left onto Chalkrow Road.

This leads you past the remains of Tower Mill (1829) on the right. At the T-junction, turn right and follow the road back to Oxborough and the start.

St John the Evangelist Church by the start is worth a visit, recently resurrected from decrepitude. The 14th-century church was built in the perpendicular style with a belltower and tall stone spire. Weakened by lightning strikes, it collapsed suddenly in 1948, leaving the building derelict.

◀ Breckland pines

Lynford Arboretum

Distance 5.5km **Time** 1 hour 45
Terrain country tracks (surfaced and
unsurfaced) **Map** OS Explorer 229
Access no public transport to the start

**Lynford Arboretum in Thetford Forest is
a Mecca for birdwatchers, with assorted
tree species attracting uncommon birds
such as hawfinches, firecrests and
crossbills. There are also bird hides
and areas of sandy beach nearby on the
banks of the flooded gravel pits of
Lynford Water.**

Start at Lynford Arboretum car park
on Lynford Road, Mundford. From the
car park, cross the road you came in on
to arrive at the Shepherds Baa café.
Opposite the café, the arboretum gateway,
with information point, takes you into
the trees. The arboretum was established
by the Forestry Commission School in
the 1950s. Note the labelled trees among
200 species.

The smooth surfaced path begins to
wind: don't double back on yourself but
head downhill. Bear left, then right,
aiming for the ponds at the bottom. Pass
a watertower as the path meanders
among meadows.

From the ponds, with the water on your
right, you arrive at a bridge. A pumphouse
on the left housed a steam-powered
engine, taking water between the ponds
and watertower to feed the hall's
decorative fountains. Cross the bridge and
keep straight ahead. Turn right where the
path peters out, then left at a gravel track.
A driveway to a private residence hidden
on the left not far along leads to the little
flint Church of our Lady of Consolation
and St Stephen (built in 1879 for the
resident of Lynford Hall).

With your back to the church and house
driveway, turn right on the gravel track to
return to the arboretum. Carry straight on
beyond a forest swing gate. The path

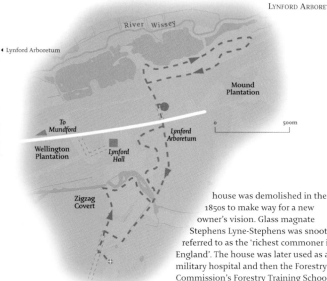

◄ Lynford Arboretum

River Wissey

Mound
Plantation

To
Mundford

Lynford
Arboretum

Wellington
Plantation

Lynford
Hall

0   500m

Zigzag
Covert

soon winds into the trees, bearing right towards a bridge leading to Lynford Hall Hotel; ignore this. Instead, follow the path beside the ponds on your left. Keep going until you reach the end of the water. A beautiful sight in summer when it is covered in waterlilies, this is always a good place to see ducks and other waterbirds. There are views of Lynford Hall, and Highland cattle sometimes graze the marshy wildflower meadows on the right.

Lynford Hall was first built around 1500 but rebuilt in 1717. In 1827 the house was remodelled again at a time when local land was cheap and aspirational Edwardians invested in shooting estates as a status symbol. This version of the house was demolished in the 1850s to make way for a new owner's vision. Glass magnate Stephens Lyne-Stephens was snootily referred to as the 'richest commoner in England'. The house was later used as a military hospital and then the Forestry Commission's Forestry Training School until 1970.

Turn left over the bridge you were on earlier to return to the arboretum, this time going straight uphill, back to the café and car park.

A post and rail gateway at the far end of the car park joins a sandy forest track to Lynford Water, a series of flooded gravel pits with sandy beaches. Quarrying revealed the area to be a Neanderthal hunting ground, with woolly mammoth remains found alongside tools such as handaxes. The lake on the left is a quiet place with bird hides but the one on the right is a popular picnic spot. You can make a circuit to the right around the grasslands before returning the way you came.

Index